A Bridge to Peradeniya

A Bridge to Peradeniya

The Adventures of a Veterinary Doctor in Sri Lanka & South India

Anand Krishnaswamy

ZERO DEGREE PUBLISHING

A Bridge to Peradeniya © Anand Krishnaswamy
First Edition by Zero Degree Publishing: March 2024

ISBN: 978-93-90053-97-1
ZDP Title: 62

This memoir was born out of the experiences of the author in veterinary college in Sri Lanka and later as a veterinary doctor working in south India and is therefore based on real patients, places, and people. The author has however, also given free rein to his imagination and some characters and places are fictitious.

ZERO DEGREE PUBLISHING
No.55(7), R Block, 6th Avenue,
Anna Nagar,
Chennai - 600 040

Website: www.zerodegreepublishing.com
E Mail id: zerodegreepublishing@gmail.com
Phone : 89250 61999

Cover Design and Illustrations by Paolo Scartaccini
Email: paoloscartaccini@gmail.com
Typeset: Vidhya Velayudham
Printed in India

To the three water buffaloes

Avantika, Vedika, & Aditya

Contents

Acknowledgements...9
Author's Note...13
Prologue...19

Part 1: A Vet Student in Kandy

Chapter One: Early Days...29
Chapter Two: The Umbrella Outside and Other Social Perils...41
Chapter Three: The Jaffna Boys...48
Chapter Four: The Kennels...62
Chapter Five: Dairy Farms...79
Chapter Six: Summer at Patuxent...84

Part 2: Lost and Found in Sri Lanka

Chapter Seven: The Charm of *Living* in Sri Lanka.......103
Chapter Eight: Pigs or Poultry, Horses or Cows?..........112
Chapter Nine: Highs and Lows...124
Chapter Ten: Guru...149
Chapter Eleven: Pregnancy Diagnosis...153
Chapter Twelve: The Peradeniya Botanical Gardens.....166

Part 3: A Newly Minted Vet in South India

Chapter Thirteen: Finding a Roof in Thoothukudi.......175
Chapter Fourteen: Pet Owners...182

Chapter Fifteen: Equine Medicine in the Nilgiris......... 195
Chapter Sixteen: Kittu 215
Chapter Seventeen: A Day at Work 225
Chapter Eighteen: Vellaiyan 239
Epilogue 258

Acknowledgements

This book took about four years to write and it was finished by 2018. After that I only made some minor changes and added one story.

It then took five years to find a publisher. I stopped keeping count after a point as it was disheartening, but by my conservative estimate, I think I probably made around 70 submissions to publishers and literary agents across the world. I resisted the free advice that was regularly given to me, to take the self-publishing route. But I must confess that I had given myself a time limit and at the start of this year, I had begun to question whether it didn't make sense to shed my customary pig-headedness and be pragmatic about this.

Writing the book was the easy part.

My gratitude to Zero Degree Publishing and Gayathri Ramasubramanian cannot be adequately captured in words. They were, in simple words, my last effort. I had decided to draw a line in the sand and stop further submissions. I am still not convinced that the self-publishing path is right for me or my writing, so this work might have remained known only to me. If you are holding this book in your hands, it is because they believed in it.

Mayuravarshini's editing with a falcon's eye for the minutest detail and her gift for understanding nuances, some of which may not even be written yet, were instrumental in the book getting its final coats of polish. Her gentle nudges and suggestions have made the work better and more rounded in its completed form. She understands the story in a holistic way and her genuine appreciation encouraged me more than she knows.

Sandhya Sridhar of Zuna Literary Agency was the one who made me believe that my random collection of stories could actually be a book. As the first one who liked my writing, I am forever grateful to her. She put me in touch with Meera Srikant who edited the first uncut versions of this work. Thank you, Meera. I know I should have paid closer attention when they were teaching us punctuation in the 7th standard.

If the faculty at the department of veterinary medicine at the University of Peradeniya had not accepted me as a student, none of this would have transpired. I could not have chased this dream without them. I will carry fond memories of my four years at Peradeniya for the rest of my life. I only have to close my eyes and I'm back on Akbar bridge.

In response to an email from a hitherto unknown person, Ranjani Rao and Nandini Patwardhan not only replied promptly, but spent a good two hours on a trans-atlantic call with me to explain the challenges and red flags to be aware of in the search for a publisher. It was on Ranjani's suggestion that I contacted Zero Degree. My thanks to both of them for their kindness.

Thank you to all those who kindly allowed me to use their names in my writing. I hope you will enjoy reading about, and in the process reliving our time together.

An excerpt from one of the chapters was published online in January 2022 by Terror House magazine. My thanks to them and to all the people who read it and sent me their kind and encouraging thoughts.

Thank you, P. R. "Guns" Ganapathy, for being such an effective sounding board and for your insights during this journey. I found a freelance artist on Upwork just like you said.

And finally a word of thanks to the universe. I continue to muddle along, usually not knowing what I'm doing, but trusting that we go where we're supposed to. But dear universe, tell us the truth. You're making this up as we go along aren't you?

Anand Krishnaswamy
30th July 2023, Cape Coral

Author's Note

This story has its genesis a few decades earlier, so let us go back to the beginning. I grew up in Madras and will always be a Madras boy. The happiest years of my life were the years I spent in school there. The friendships that took root during those years when we were all children remain strong and endure now, decades later.

My love for animals and science began when I was a young boy, my hero at that time being Gerald Durrell. His stories of animal-collecting expeditions to exotic locales captivated me, and in my own humble and haphazard way, I collected grasshoppers, beetles, spiders, and frogs to keep as pets. Later, my favourite author was James Herriot who wrote so beautifully about being a veterinarian in rural England.

As is common to young people, I spent several years being confused about the direction I wanted to take in my career. I wanted to be a naturalist, start a zoo, go on wildlife expeditions, and be a marine biologist, all at once. It was only when I reached my second year of undergraduate college in Madras – I got my first degree in Botany – that realisation dawned, that veterinary medicine was my calling, no doubt influenced by my volunteering experiences at the Blue Cross, an animal shelter in Chennai. The magical world that James Herriot had created in my imagination ultimately triumphed over all other fantasies.

By that time, I had decided that I wanted to go to the U.S.A. for postgraduate studies. "Okay," I thought to myself, "Let's go get a veterinary degree in the U.S."

I thought it was so simple. From the basic research I did, I knew that U.S. veterinary colleges required several pre-requisite courses in order to qualify, which I lacked. So I decided that I would first get to the U.S. and then worry about doing the required courses. After all, wasn't the U.S. the country where merit and hard work could take you wherever you wanted?

I applied and got into a master's course in Zoology at a university in Florida. It was only after landing there that reality hit me. And how! At that time, veterinary courses cost about 35,000 to 45,000 dollars per year and there was no possibility of getting a scholarship. There was simply no way I could afford the course and there was the additional cost of taking all the social science courses that I lacked to qualify, which would be an additional expense.

So there I was, stuck in a strange country, in a course that held no interest for me, and with the feeling that I had made my long-suffering parents spend a huge sum of money, all for nothing. After a few weeks of weeping over this, I knew I had to do something. I could either go back home, or transfer to another course.

Arizona State University (ASU) had a master's course in agribusiness that seemed job-oriented, and that I qualified for. In addition, one of my closest friends, a neighbour from Madras, was already there studying for his master's degree in engineering. I badly needed a friend and it seemed like a good idea, even though I had never heard the word 'agribusiness' before that point. I sent an email to the Dean of the Agribusiness department, and he invited me over for a visit. That was enough for me and I hopped on a Greyhound bus that took two days to go from Florida on the east coast, to Arizona on the west coast of the U.S.A. My friends still joke that I am the only person on earth who has travelled the interstate freeway I-10 from end to end.

The move to ASU was a smash hit in every sense. After the initial five months of misery, seeing my friend Naini who came to pick me up at the Greyhound bus station at Tempe, Arizona, was pure joy. Hootie and the Blowfish had just topped the charts and their song 'Hold My Hand' played on the car's radio in the lead singer's gravelly voice as we drove out under the Tempe sun. About a year previously, I had met one of Naini's undergraduate classmates, Pattabhiraman, in Madras. Patta had also joined Naini at ASU and was the first person to greet me when I reached their apartment.

There were 30 or 40 boys from Madras studying at ASU, and they all lived in that apartment. I met them all in the next few days and also met the Dean of the Agribusiness department, who took about ten minutes to grant me admission to the programme. My hand felt held. I was happy.

And so my dream of becoming a vet was put into a box, shelved and forgotten, while I settled down into college life at ASU and enjoyed myself with a vengeance. Patta, Naini and I moved into an apartment, and I will always cherish the few years that we spent together in Tempe, before they found jobs, then partners, married, and moved into their own spaces and lives.

I eventually graduated with a master's degree in agribusiness and started working for a fruit exporting and distributing company. But soon, the pull of home became too strong to ignore and I bought myself a one-way ticket back to my beloved Madras, which was now called Chennai.

It was the correct move for me, and I was deeply happy to be back in my hometown. I was not sure about the kind of work I wanted to do, but a little over a year after moving back, I found work as an independent development consultant and did that for the next decade.

And it was around now that the genie of my veterinary dream escaped from the box that I had packed it into and pushed deep into the dusty attic of my mind. I was thoroughly enjoying my work and the independence that it offered me. I was travelling the world and earning well... and yet, there was this nagging feeling that this was not really what I was meant to do. That maybe, just maybe, I had given up on my dream too easily.

In the project I worked on, we helped entrepreneurs with innovative technologies set up businesses so that their ideas could impact the larger community. Most of them were deeply committed to their ideas and I was both humbled and inspired to work with them. Perhaps that was what pushed me to think about my own calling again.

Over the next few years, I toyed with my dream like a lemming. I would write to universities and ask about their veterinary programmes and meet professors to express my interest. But I would always go all the way to the cliff edge, peer down at the churning ocean, and then be too scared to make the leap.

In this manner, I went back and forth for several years, causing myself a great deal of angst and pain. But the genie was out of the box and would not go back in, no matter how much I reasoned and argued with him. The lemming had truly got into me. In the end, I jumped.

I took admission into a veterinary college in Sri Lanka and set off on an adventure that would last four years and beyond.

These are some stories of my journey through veterinary college there and my first years as a vet in south India. They speak of the sometimes infuriating, sometimes wonderful, but always interesting animals and humans I met along the way. Some experiences left me crushed, others uplifted me. In short, it was a deep dive into life.

It is from those cherished and unforgettable experiences that this book was born.

Anand Krishnaswamy
4th May 2020, Chennai

Prologue

On Tuesday mornings, from 10.15 AM to 12.15 PM in my first semester of veterinary college, at the University of Peradeniya, we had clinical rotations at the university farm and at the teaching hospital which took primarily dog and cat cases. If this week our class was at the farm, then the next week it would be at the hospital.

It was mostly about learning the basics of handling and examining animals, becoming comfortable around them, and getting a feel for what the profession was like. I thoroughly enjoyed those classes, because for me, at last, after what seemed like never-ending hours of lectures, I was finally among animals. I had heard horror stories that we students wouldn't handle animals until our final year. So I was thrilled that we had such structured practical learning in the very first year. The best way to learn, after all, is by doing.

On one such sunny Tuesday morning in December, we were at the hospital again. It seemed to be especially busy that morning, perhaps because of the long weekend that had just ended, due to poya day falling on Monday. The outpatient ward was full of dogs of varying sizes, some lying prone on examination tables, others on the floor, next to their owners. Doctors were rushing about in the usual chaos of the hospital, and following our introductory lecture by the instructor, we were let loose among the people and their pets.

Veterinarians call it the per-rectal exam. The rectum is one of the preferred places to check temperature in animals, so vets stick thermometers into almost every animal they handle as part of the initial evaluation of the patient. Dogs especially, seem to be prone to a variety of ailments that require a rectal examination. One of the most common complaints that owners bring their pets in for, is to have the anal sacs cleared.

The anal sacs are two little glands that sit on either side at the four o'clock and eight o'clock positions of the rectum. They produce a mucous secretion that under normal circumstances lubricates the faeces during defecation.

But when they get infected, or when there is an impaction, the secretions remain inside and create great discomfort and pain to the dog. It's the vet's job to clear them out at such times.

It's a skill that all veterinarians must learn. During some of our earlier visits, I had observed doctors doing it without really knowing why. And I had been disgusted and repelled.

I mean, it's one thing to stick a thermometer into a dog's anus and quite another to put your own finger in.

I suppose we should have known that there was something nasty brewing when the doctor-on-call summoned us around his case and told the attendant to "...bring some gloves."

"Do you know how to do a per-rectal exam?" he asked.

Anybody watching would have seen the smooth Mexican wave with which we all involuntarily stepped back from the table with perfect coordination.

Pulling on his gloves, the doctor lifted the tail of the big Rottweiler on the table with his left hand. Sticking out his right index finger, he pushed it all the way into the anus.

I was right next to the doctor, with the crush of my classmates crowded around the table. Sensing a sudden commotion behind me, I turned around and saw that one girl had fainted and was sliding to the floor. Some of my more alert classmates caught her.

Three of them lifted her up and the whole group started moving like a funeral procession to take her out of the ward.

"Let's wait for them to come back," said the doctor, extracting his finger. Then he himself stepped out to attend to the girl and the rest of us followed. She was laid out on the chairs next to the pharmacy and some of her friends stayed with her until she recovered.

Back at the Rottweiler table, the examination continued. One by one, we put on our gloves and did what the doctor did, while he watched and instructed us about what to feel for, and where to search with our finger for the anal sac.

When my turn came, I adopted the strategy of shutting out all repulsive thoughts and focussing purely on the biology. "It's a tissue," I told myself. "Now you're feeling the sphincter... oh, is that the gluteal muscle?"

Once past the sphincter, which strained reflexively against my finger, I felt some solid structures moving against it. "I can feel something moving. Are these the sacs?" I asked the doctor.

"Let's see," he said as I removed my finger, and he inserted his again.

"Those are not anal sacs but faecal matter," he said calmly.

"Oh shit," I said, unable to control my emotions.

"Yes, that's correct," he replied sotto voce, motioning the next person to step forward and have a feel.

—

Soon after our stint at the teaching hospital, we first years found ourselves at the university farm, and the lesson for the day was on handling and examining cows. We were gathered around the cattle barn that had about six cows on either side of the food trough, looking at us with interest as we got our lecture.

Our instructor was a junior teacher who had recently graduated from the course – a few of them had been hired to function as teaching assistants, handle farm and hospital practical classes, and assist in anatomy, physiology and biochemistry practicals. As they were young, we students found them less intimidating to approach when we had questions or wanted some help. Also, they seemed to remember their own first-year experiences only too well and were ever-willing to help and advise us on practical matters like preparation for our exams. In short, they were a terrific resource, which we students took full advantage of.

"Do any of you know what the right method to restrain a cow for examination is?" he asked.

When it was clear that none of us had any idea, he continued.

"You have to insert your fingers into the cow's nose and pinch the nasal septum. The cow will feel pain and stop struggling.

We will try with this cow," he said, indicating a smallish cow that was standing at the end of the barn. She was about half the size of her companions.

He stepped up to her, and holding one of her horns, he pulled her head around. Then, he inserted his thumb and forefinger into her nose and pinched. Sure enough, the poor cow became quite still after that.

"But wouldn't that stress the animal?" I asked.

"Yes, it does cause it some stress, but this is the accepted method to restrain the cow for clinical examinations," he replied.

"Okay, who will be the first to try?" he asked. I put my hand up and stepped up next to the cow. Rubbing her back and talking to her, I grasped her horn and tried to pull her head around as he had done.

For such a small cow, she was surprisingly strong and resisted my efforts. But huffing and puffing, and using both my hands, I managed to pull her head around. Next, putting my thumb and forefinger into her nose as I had seen him do, I pinched the septum, which felt a lot like the cartilage in our own noses, only thicker. Nothing happened. The cow continued to try to pull her head away.

"You have to pinch hard," he said.

Cringing inwardly, I slowly increased the pressure. It worked, and the cow became still.

"Okay, good. Now put your leg up on the railing and place her head on your knee. Hold it there," he instructed. I did as I was told, and the teacher called the rest of the students one by one to check the heart sounds of the cow and to listen for abdominal sounds.

With mild surprise, I noticed that I was breathing heavily. Large animal work is hard physical labour. And all I had done was pinch a small cow's nasal septum and put her head on my knee!

One by one, the students tried their hand at pinching that poor cow's nose. I remember hoping that none of the girls had long nails because nobody was checking. I really felt bad for that cow, but I needn't have worried.

She was quite capable of taking care of herself.

The next class at the farm came around a fortnight later. Again, we had to restrain a cow. Again, the instructor chose the same cow to be our practice animal.

But this time she was ready. When I approached her, she put her head down and attempted to mock butt me. There was no real danger there, but the message was clear – "Leave me alone."

When I persisted, she refused to let me reach her nose by cleverly putting her head down and keeping it away from reach, no matter how much I tried. I used all my strength to pull her head around, but she proved stronger.

While we kept trying, she brought out a new move. She simply turned around in her place and presented her backside to us. If we squeezed past her to reach the head, she would turn around another 180 degrees. Every now and then, she would try butting us with her horns.

The instructor knew when to give up. "This cow is too aggressive," he said. "Let's try with another cow."

The same thing happened in later classes as well, whenever we went to the cow barn and had to handle cows. We always had to work with other animals, since this particular cow never let us restrain her again. Like most people, I had thought that cows were slightly dumb creatures, and that they would submit to any kind of human handling. One encounter with inexperienced first year students putting their fingers into her nose was enough for her. Not only did she remember that experience, she never let it happen again.

PART 1

A Vet Student in Kandy

Chapter One

Early Days

When I decided to attend veterinary school in Sri Lanka, I tried to mentally prepare myself for a lot of things. I knew it would be hard to sit in lecture halls for extended periods after working for so many years. I wondered if I would have to spend a lot on things like rent and books, and how I would manage my savings to cover all such expenses. Underneath the brave face I put on, I wondered if I would be able to cope with the course. I had generally never had a problem with academics through all my school and college years, but at that point, I had been sitting in comfortable offices, working, for more than a decade. I wondered if I had gone soft, if I could still do it.

But then, there was a whole range of things that I simply could not have prepared myself for. Society in Sri Lanka is still conservative, and if anything, this is exacerbated in a small town like Kandy where my college was. I suspect I was the first foreign student in the history of the veterinary department, and thus, a novelty for everyone. My first interaction with my classmates was on the topic of my dress sense, or – as they saw it – the lack thereof.

I had observed with mild surprise that medical and veterinary students in this university came to college dressed in formals. Curiously, this only applied to boys; girls dressed as they pleased in colourful skirts, tops and pants. But the boys always turned up in plain white or light-coloured formal shirts and full dark trousers with black shoes.

I rarely dressed in formals, even when I was a working professional in my life before entering veterinary college. I had gone to Kandy with a wardrobe of two pairs of corduroys, one pair of jeans and some cotton shirts.

Two days after I landed, I was accosted in the canteen by a boy, while waiting for my breakfast order. "From tomorrow, you will dress like us," he blurted out.

"Why?" I replied.

He took a few seconds to digest that one.

"We are in a professional course, so we have to dress like professionals," he said.

I decided that this was not the time to quiz him on what he understood by professionalism. Instead I answered: "These are all the clothes I have, so this is how I'll dress."

The same scene replayed about three or four times with different people, either singly or in groups, telling me that my dressing style was not acceptable. On one occasion, a group of five boys surrounded me and said that they would take me to the market to purchase the appropriate clothes if I didn't have any. "Will you also pay?" I asked, upon which they withdrew to reassess their strategy.

It was becoming very tiresome, and definitely not something I needed in my first week of life there, when other adjustments were difficult enough. Later, these same classmates became my good friends, but my relationship with them started on a hostile note.

College education is free for Sri Lankans and unfortunately, I landed there right in the middle of an ongoing island-wide student agitation. Student unions across the country were protesting against the government's proposal to allow private colleges. In their collective view, this would create a situation where private colleges would lure away the best teachers by offering them higher salaries, while those students who could not afford the fees would be left with a lower quality of education in the public, government-aided colleges.

To the seniors in my department, many of whom were active in the student unions, I was Public Enemy Number One. I epitomised everything they thought they were fighting against. I tried to explain to them that my presence there was completely legitimate, that the university had a quota for foreign students, and that I had not stolen any seat from a Sri Lankan student. But they paid no heed. I was like a made-to-order target for their misdirected energy, so why bother with things like introspection or reason?

Like a shadowy mafia, those seniors spread their influence through the student body and made sure that I felt their presence throughout the four years of my student life at Peradeniya.

The veterinary department had a tradition where seniors would sometimes organise preparatory sessions called 'kuppis' for juniors prior to exams. They would contain general advice on how to prepare for them and helpful tips on important topics and so on. I came to know of this practice just before our first semester exams, when one of my classmates invited me to go with her to attend it. "It will be helpful in our preparation," she told me. I agreed and accompanied her to the classroom where all my friends had assembled. A group of seniors was at the front and one of them was writing something on the board.

The moment they saw me, a hush fell in the room. They huddled together and the classmate who had invited me to the session was called up. A quick discussion later, she walked back to me looking embarrassed and miserable.

It was not difficult to understand what was going on. There would be no kuppi that day if I was in attendance. Thanking my friend for inviting me and telling her not to worry about it, I left.

The story repeated itself several times and in varying contexts over the next four years.

Another much-loved tradition of the veterinary faculty was the Annual Gala. The entire department including the students, support staff and professors looked forward to this event. It was organised by the third years and a tremendous amount of preparation seemed to go into them, with sponsors being solicited, a magazine being published, bookings made at a star hotel and so on. In the weeks leading up to the grand party, the excitement would infect even the professors and they would talk about it in class.

I heard several stories about how this was the one time when even some of our stricter professors would let their hair down and mingle with students. They must have been fun, but I would never know because it was made very clear to me that I was not welcome there. Not even when we were in our third year and it was my own classmates who were doing all the organising. And not in our fourth year when we were all going through the grind of clinical rotations at the hospital and farm, when I thought that we had truly bonded as a group.

It was as if my classmates were always aware of the seniors' presence somewhere behind their backs. They would not stand up to them and say, "He is one of us."

Unlike my classmates who soon warmed up to me, the seniors carefully nursed their hostility towards me. Till the very end, whenever they saw me on campus, I would feel their glares and comments following me.

In that same first week on campus, a group of third-year students surrounded my table at the canteen one morning, like a scene from a movie. It was very dramatic. After asking me who I was and where I was from, and how much fees I had paid, they made their dislike of me crystal clear. "It's a problem for us," they declared, "that you are in our department." They simply couldn't take the idea of a first-year student who knew his own mind and didn't even acknowledge them, never mind being cowed down. And one who came to college in sneakers and checked shirts to boot.

They actually took their protest about me to the Dean and asked him how he had allowed a foreigner to enter the faculty. Later, he told me that he had to explain that the university had a quota for foreign students and that my admission was valid. "But they also protested about your dressing style, and there, I agree with them," he said. "Why don't you dress like them, tuck your shirt in and wear a belt?" he asked.

"At this stage in my life, I really don't need anyone to tell me how to dress," I responded. "And besides, they are only talking about professionalism. I have lived it before coming here."

The Dean's reply was diplomatic. He said, "But when you are in a new country, shouldn't you try to be like the locals?"

I knew when to take a step back. And he had been on my side all along. "Of course, I understand. I'll make an effort, but I cannot dress exactly like them," I said, which he agreed to.

After that episode, I went to college in the same half-sleeved cotton shirts and shapeless corduroys and jeans. But I kept the promise I made to the Dean. I made sure my shirt was always tucked in.

—

Tests were very much part of the first year of my veterinary course. We had three subjects that year – Anatomy, Physiology and Biochemistry. While starting the year, I had imagined that I would have the most difficulty with biochemistry, because my fundamentals were weak – I had never really paid attention in high school and topics like the Kreb's Cycle still make my eyes glaze over.

But no, it was anatomy that proved to be the biggest challenge, simply because of the sheer volume of subject matter and the depth of detail that we had to know.

In the biochemistry and physiology tests, it was a matter of preparing and simply taking them. The teacher would test us at the end of each chapter, because of which there was somehow not too much stress associated with them. If you failed, it was no big deal; it didn't go on your record. Yes, they did display the names and scores on the department's notice board, open to anyone who wanted to check. I remember one notable occasion when for a particularly hard test I got a zero. I consoled myself because several of my classmates actually managed to get negative marks on that test. To my overactive imagination, when I saw my score on the notice board, neon lights and highlighted asterisks seemed to flash only next to my name.

In the early weeks we would all rush to the notice board the moment word got around that the marks were out. But soon, we became hardened soldiers. Getting a low score became something to boast about... I once overheard this conversation when those marks came out, between a male classmate and a group of girls he was chatting with.

"Hey, Jayantha, how about your physiology marks?" asked one of the girls.

Jayantha puffed out his chest and grinned widely. "I got minus five!" he said.

"Oahhhhhhwwww," chorused the girls, eyes dancing and white teeth showing in a blaze of pretty smiles.

For those five minutes, Jayantha was Zorro, the masked bandit.

But anatomy was different. The tests were oral. They divided us into groups of five and we were tested as a group. Looking back now, I realise that it was great practice for the many viva voce tests that we would take in the future, but at that time, I only remember what nerve-wracking experiences they were.

They were actually pencilled into the semester schedule of practical classes, so we had enough and more time to prepare. The results of these oral tests didn't go on our records either, but somehow the whole experience of being grilled for three hours along with your peers made them heavier and more serious... it definitely wasn't okay to get a low grade.

Grades of C or lower generally earned you genuine sympathy and murmured commiseration.

We tried to surreptitiously help each other out in spite of the teacher being five feet away. But you still felt ashamed if you were not able to answer most of the questions thrown at you.

No matter how much you prepared, it was never enough. You knew that there would be a googly or two coming your way from some section that you had not managed to cover.

The digestive system was one such section that we were tested on, early in the second semester. In anatomy, the digestive system covers everything from the point where the food enters the animal's mouth, to the point where it comes out at the other end.

The day of the test arrived and my head was full of facts. I had prepared so hard that I felt like I had turned into a gut bacterium myself and done a safari through the gastrointestinal tract.

There were six of us in the group, and the professor went around the table in rotation, asking each of us questions in turn. Eventually it was my turn, and as the professor tilted his chin and raised his eyebrow slightly at me, I sat up a little straighter.

"Anand," said the professor, "tell me, what is the position of the rumen in the abdominal cavity?"

It was a gentle off break, flighted up outside the off stump. I defended with bat and pad close to each other.

"The rumen is on the left side of the median plane, between the eighth rib and pelvic recess," I replied. "It extends from the top to the bottom of the abdominal cavity."

"Where can you palpate the rumen?"

Another easy ball, pitched up on middle-and-leg. This is my day, I thought as I answered, "At the para lumbar fossa."

Time to step out and tonk his next ball over the long on boundary.

"Tell me," said the professor, suddenly changing tack, "what is the function of the Paneth cells of the jejunum?"

It was the googly.

Like all good bowlers, he had saved it to be used as a surprise weapon – I was caught completely off guard and comprehensively bowled.

—

All through that first year of the veterinary course, we had anatomy dissection lab, which I never really enjoyed. During one of these Wednesday afternoon lab sessions, my group was dissecting a dog's forelimb. We were hunched over the dog's cadaver when our teachers came to check on our progress.

"Look at this, they have cut the brachial artery," exclaimed a teacher to a colleague in a tone of rising disappointment. "What happened? Normally you people are more careful, no?" she asked us. And off they went to the next table and the next group.

I looked at my group mates as we shared the nervous smiles of the clueless. I gripped the sides of the table. “Deep breath,” I told myself, “Deep breath.”

Dissection of the Dog by Evans & de la Hunta was our bible and book of deliverance. It was a lovely book, with all the major organ systems and parts of the dog neatly laid out in sequential chapters. The text was written in simple enough language, even if the amount of detail was intimidating. But by then, I had reached the point where I was saying, “This is anatomy, what do you expect?”

The illustrations in the book were copious and superb, but there was only one issue. When you opened up the dog, it bore little resemblance to all those neatly labelled and coloured diagrams. It was mostly just an amorphous mass of tissue, bones and vasculature. If we were able (after an hour of cutting and constant reference to our textbook) to identify one muscle from the mass, there would be a minor wave of triumph around the dissection table. But we quickly learned to keep such victories quiet. In one early instance, we had called the teacher over to show her.

“Very good,” she said, “So now you have the rhomboideus.”

And before we could start smiling, the next question was fired at me.

“What are the attachments?”

As I squirmed in discomfort and ignorance, she turned to another member of my group.

“Okay, can you tell me what are the nerves that innervate this muscle?”

As the silence extended uncomfortably and we looked fixedly at the cadaver, she said, "Check, check your textbook... you people should know this," and moved on to the next table.

We knew that the dog's anatomy was a big part of our end-semester exams. Just in case we forgot, the assistant teachers would remind us constantly, "Dog dissection is one of the mooosst important topics in your exam... make sure you understand it well."

Well, thank you.

Our teachers were kind to us. They meant well, they wanted us to learn, and that's why they pushed us. Another time, we were in gross anatomy lab, studying the bones of the shoulder joint and limbs. Up came our teacher and began to quiz us about the specimens on the table.

Picking up a hoof she asked, "To whom does this belong?"

"A horse," I said.

"Oh, very good!" she exclaimed. "And how did you identify it?"

"Oh... it just looks like a horse's hoof," I replied lamely.

"It looks like..." she said but couldn't complete her sentence as she collapsed in laughter. Once she recovered, she pointed out the obvious fact that the horse's hoof is the only one that is not cleaved in two. It's one piece, compared to bovine or porcine hooves that have two 'toes'.

Next, picking up a mounted specimen of a scapula and its attendant foreleg from another table, she asked, "Okay, whose is this?" Her smile kept getting wider as we made one wild guess after another. Finally, giving up on us, she said, "It's a pig! You people think too much, you are looking for tiny details when you miss the most obvious clues... look at the scapula! I even turned it on the lateral side so you people would see the spine!"

I wanted to kick myself. The pig's scapula has a spine on its lateral side that curves like a surfer's wave. You cannot miss it... if you remember to look for it.

"I want you people to pick up these skills..." she said, as she walked away smiling.

In spite of my growing appreciation for the lab, I was still overwhelmed by the sheer enormity of detail. If only we didn't have to know the attachment, innervations, arteries and veins for each and every muscle. The pressure of having to know all that detail took away the joy of learning.

At the same time, I was aware that someday in the future, if I made it as a veterinarian, I would probably use this knowledge, or at the very least, know where to look for it in the Dissection of the Dog.

Chapter Two

The Umbrella Outside and Other Social Perils

The University of Peradeniya is blessed with soul-stirring natural beauty. The copious rain, the cool climate of the hills, and the abundant sunlight during the dry periods combine to make a heady combination that drives plants mad with joy. This has made the hill town of Kandy, where the university is located, the verdant retreat that it is.

I always loved walking the serene roads of the university, hemmed in on all sides by overflowing vegetation. I could never get enough of the enormous, majestic trees that stood at practically every corner. Those trees were a treasure trove that nobody seemed to notice. When you are surrounded by riches, I suppose you start taking them for granted. At times, when I thought nobody was looking, I'd just put my hand on their trunks and stand next to them for a few minutes, with what I'm sure was a mildly loopy expression on my face.

Then there were the century-old buildings and architecture of the university that somehow did not encroach on the natural beauty, but seemed to enhance it.

At several locations in those rolling hills, were strategically-placed little outhouses. I don't know what their original purpose was, other than perhaps as a resting place for people walking those paths, or maybe to shelter from the rain, which was never too far away. They were all of the same design: circular structures, with a diameter of maybe six or seven steps, with domed roofs and large windows on all sides. They were made from stone and had large entrances. The entrances and the windows were created as openings in the stone walls.

Those innocent-looking resting spots however, played a much deeper role in the social life of the university students. This was explained to me one day as I walked the grounds with my classmates. We were near the Central Administration Block – a particularly beautiful area with green lawns and trees, with massive ground-level branches. My friends pointed out a pathway meandering away into the distance.

"Do you know what that is?" one of them asked.

"No, where does it go?" I asked in return.

"That is the Lover's Walk," came the reply.

"Well, that makes sense," I thought to myself. It was only natural that students would be drawn to this lovely spot for their amorous interludes. And here was a pathway that might as well have been made-to-order for them. Fairy-tale-like, there was even a brook gurgling alongside. To top it all, those superb branches spreading out all over the lawn, creating secluded nooks, were ideal for any sort of romancing. It was perfect.

"See that outhouse over there?" asked another friend, pointing to a familiar domed structure, which was some distance along Lover's Walk.

"Do you know what happens there?" this, with a gleam appearing in his eye.

"What?" I asked, guessing what was coming.

"It's for couples to go inside and do whatever they want."

"What do you mean whatever they want?"

"I mean – whatever they want," this was delivered with emphasis and a pitying look.

"When you see an umbrella outside the entrance, it means there is a couple inside, and you should not disturb them. Only university students are allowed on this Lover's Walk and only they can use the outhouses," explained my friend.

"If you are studying here, you can bring your boyfriend or girlfriend even if they are not students, but outsiders are not allowed," he went on, looking earnestly at me to see if I understood this subtle variation of the unwritten law.

I nodded seriously and made appropriate noises to show that I did.

"But why do you need that umbrella? You can easily see inside through the windows and the entrance if there is someone inside, right?" I couldn't resist asking.

I got more pitying looks. 'How did they allow a fellow with such low I.Q. into our university?' they seemed to ask.

I never got an answer to that question.

During my first five months, I lived at the top of a hill – a walk that took me beside an outhouse that was popular due to its location away from the university's main campus. I walked past it every day, and on several occasions, I noticed couples sitting on the windowsills and enjoying an evening date. But not once, not even during the times I had to walk up late at night, did I spot that umbrella that carried so significant a meaning.

—

As you descend the hill atop where I lived, there was a residence hall just abutting the college campus where I used to spend a good chunk of my time on weekends. There were several good reasons to do so. One, it had a mess. So stopping there for food on my way up the hill made sense (and on weekends, I had to come down to the campus to eat anyway). Second, they often had last month's English newspapers laid out on their reading stand. There was a study hall with tables and chairs and nice large windows. Finally, there was a TV in the mess, where, if I was lucky, some Indian channel would be playing, or a cricket match would be on.

They didn't seem to mind me eating there, or even studying in the hall, even though I'm pretty certain they knew I didn't live there. Often, the resident troop of Purple-faced leaf-eating monkeys would come out to forage in the small garden in front of the mess, and it was fun to watch them.

On one occasion, I had just finished eating when some student switched on the TV. India's test match against the West Indies at the Wankhede stadium had just ended. Sachin Tendulkar was making his farewell speech. It was very unexpected and I was completely unprepared for the emotions that swept over me as I realised that I would never see Sachin play in India's colours again.

Our heroes seep insidiously into our lives. As Sachin started his career with that test series in Pakistan - the same one in which Waqar Younis sent down the bouncer in Sialkot that broke his 16 - year - old nose - and later as he grew into a master batsman and smashed all records, I finished school and college, moved to the U.S. for higher studies and started on my career. Those were the years when the journey started…of leaving the cocoon of parents and home, of friendship, of heartbreak, of self-discovery and becoming an adult. Through it all, cricket was always in the background, a passion unaffected by the happenings in life. And so, naturally, was Sachin Tendulkar. Sachin's retirement signalled an end to that part of my own life. I suppose it was the combination of where I was in my life at that time – in more ways than simply my physical location – that brought on the reaction. I was trying my best to remain unwavering in spite of my nervousness at my leap into the unknown, and the difficulties of adapting to my changed circumstances.

He had some written notes clutched in his hand, but he did not look at them even once. When you speak from the heart, you rarely need notes. And so, as Sachin spoke the touching words of farewell, I couldn't stop the tears from flowing. Luckily there were only a few students eating at that time, and they were mostly behind me, so I hoped nobody would notice. I tried my best to quietly wipe the tears away from the corners of my eyes, pretending to brush my face with my hand.

Once the speech was finished, I picked up my backpack to leave, and swung my legs around from underneath the long trestle table.

Right there, to my left, sat a student trying his best to avert his gaze – I realised he had probably missed Sachin's entire speech, finding instead, my performance far more interesting. There was nothing much left to do, other than exit as quickly as possible.

Luckily, that was one of my last weekends there. I found a better house on the other side of the town, and my territorial prowling moved to a different area very soon after that incident. Mercifully, I never went back to that mess again.

—

It was fish biology and aquaculture class on a Friday morning early in my third semester. Fridays were good that semester because, although we had to sit through two two-hour long lectures, that was all we had. We were free in the afternoons, a luxury not to be taken casually.

After he passed around the attendance sheet, the teacher began by asking a question. "Last class, we studied the different types of skin and its functions based on the different species, habitats, etc. Who can tell me the classification of scales in fish?"

"Shshwooshmooshkoosh... placoid... gooshshhoosshmooosh," came the chorus of forty whispered answers from behind my back, sounding like an army of fat rats running through a grassy field.

"Eh," said the professor in his habitual style. "I can't hear you."

Again, "Mwooshhooshkoosh... pointed... sca... eeesh moooshooooshh." The rats were doing a full circuit of the field.

By this time, I realised that my hands were gripping the sides of my chair... I dearly wanted to stand up, turn around and scream, "Can't you speak properly instead of whispering, you morons?"

If I'd done that, I know exactly what the response would have been, accompanied by shy smiles, downturned eyes, coy looks, the full act, "Noooshwoosh... he he ha ha… boooshvooosh... ha ha… oooshhhshhh."

This was the time to start my deep breathing exercises, because otherwise, I was seconds away from attacking whoever was next to me with my ball point pen. It drove me crazy. Many a time, I would answer just to pre-empt the irritating whisper brigade behind me.

It had been a full year since we had started veterinary school as a batch. This same professor had taught us other subjects. And the same scene played out again and again, with nary a change. He would ask a question. There would be an outbreak of whispers. And he would say, "Eh? I can't hear you!" Whereupon the whispers would start afresh.

Eventually he would provide the answer himself and carry on with the lesson.

Until he thought of asking another question.

Chapter Three

The Jaffna Boys

It was a sunny morning in the first week of November. It was the second year of our course and we had just finished our third semester-ending microbiology exam. The usual procedure was for us to wait in our seats for about fifteen minutes after an exam while the invigilators collected our papers, counted them and ensured that everything was in order.

I leaned back in my seat with a sigh, thinking about question number seven – 'Name a bacterium that causes Otitis externa in the dog.' For the life of me, I hadn't been able to recall the answer. There is nothing more annoying than that sliver of detail that teases you from just beyond the reaches of your memory.

When Thileepan, a Tamil boy sitting in front of me turned around, I asked him, "Eppaddi pan'ninenga?" – "How did you do?"

"Yetho pan'nen," he said with a grin, which translates as – "I managed" – but which meant he hadn't done well.

"Yen, yenna aachu?" I asked. – "Why, what happened?"

"Padikkal'e..." he laughed as he answered. – "I didn't study..."

I joined in the laugh. What else could I do? I had spent weeks losing sleep over an exam and here was a classmate who hadn't even bothered to study and seemed nonchalant about it!

They were a gang of five Tamil boys in our class that year – I called them the Jaffna boys even though only Thileepan and Makinthan were from there. Ashraf was from Mannar, Murugan was from Vavuniya and Senthil had his home in Trincomalee.

They were on some trip of their own, those boys. While the rest of us struggled through classes and labs, each day bringing with it some new stress about a test, or the need to photocopy lab instructions for the next day, the Jaffna boys laughed and joked their way through it all.

They sat in the last row. Two of them spoke a smattering of Sinhala, but they mostly stuck to Tamil, since that was the only language they knew. If the teachers asked them anything, they replied in halting, broken English. It was a little sad – despite being Sri Lankan, in many ways they were as foreign as I was.

They spoke to me in Tamil and while I could understand most of their dialect, at times it was difficult, as Sri Lankan Tamils speak a more classical form of the language than the Madras patois. Murugan, in particular, had such a thick accent that for the entire first two months, I was convinced that he had been drinking before class.

Very often, I would find them missing. When I queried them on their absence, they would explain how they had been busy raising funds for the Pongal celebration at the faculty, or preparing idlis for a pooja at the local Hindu temple. At other times, it was because a friend had come to town and they had thrown an impromptu party. I suspected that most of the time, it was the parties that kept them away from the class. After all, if you drink late into the night, how can you attend a parasitology lecture at 8 AM?

It was a wonder to me how they managed to pass the exams at all. But pass they did, very often on the second or third attempt, using a formula that combined sourcing past question papers from senior students, some strategic planning about which parts to study and which ones to leave out, feverish memorisation of the material, and plain, old-fashioned luck. I envied them but never had the courage to adopt their methods, not even for our mid-term exams. And with their happy-go-lucky ways, they were popular and everyone seemed to enjoy their company.

One of the first things that struck me as I was getting to know them was a quaint behavioural trait of doing pretty much everything together... including visiting the washroom. They arrived in the morning from their hostel together, ate their meals together, and spent whatever free time we had drinking tea together in the canteen. So I suppose it was only natural that they also went to the restroom as one.

Once during those early days, they invited me to join them. Since it was a class of 75 students, we were divided into four batches for laboratory classes due to the space constraint. I was in the same batch as the Jaffna boys. One day, while waiting for the earlier batch to finish Microbiology lab, the boys started drifting away.

Turning to me, Makinthan asked: “Bass, varengl'a?” – “Boss, are you coming?”

"Enge?" I asked. "Where?"

He held up his pinky finger in a gesture that is common to the south of India as well as Sri Lanka, as I discovered that day.

"Urine pfass," he declared.

I politely declined the invitation. But I was thinking, "Really, guys, do you need company even to take a leak?"

An uncommon bond grew between Makinthan and me. We were about as far apart as it's possible on life's spectrum, and I doubt if we would have found any common ground if not for the fact that we were both veterinary students.

Here was a boy whose world before veterinary college had been the Indian Ocean lagoons and palm trees of rural north Sri Lanka. He had grown up in the midst of a civil war that had ravaged that part of the country and its people. Being a veterinary student was for him, already, an achievement, since he was the first in his family to attend college. His dream was to finish college, return to Jaffna and join the government's Animal Health division.

On one occasion he mentioned an uncle who had emigrated to Canada and a possibility of going there. But from his tone, it was clear that he believed that to be a fantasy. Reality was the government job.

And here I was, a city-born and bred Indian. Veterinary college was, for me, a hiatus, an adventure, a dream that I was chasing. I had absolutely no idea where I would end up after school or what I would do, but I had about fifteen different fantasies that ranged from becoming a volunteer vet in Costa Rica, to specialising in small animal orthopaedics – and I loved them all.

One day, we were visiting the health centre to get our mandatory anti-rabies vaccination. While walking back we started talking about his life in Jaffna and he casually mentioned being conscripted in the war, literally stopping me in my tracks.

He told the story in a matter-of-fact way, devoid of any melodrama or exaggerated self-pity.

The events happened in the year 2009, as the Tamil rebels fighting the government made their last stand at Mullaitivu in northern Sri Lanka. Makinthan, along with his father, mother and three brothers, was in the refugee camp along with thousands of other Tamil people. One elder brother had already been forcefully conscripted and had died fighting.

One afternoon, his mother was cooking in an open stove outside their dwelling and his father was standing nearby, when the army started shelling the camp. Even as they scrambled to get to the safe zone, his father was hit by shrapnel. Makinthan explained how it left a huge gaping wound on his abdomen and he collapsed. They tried their best to get him medical aid but he did not survive.

On another occasion, he was strolling along the beach with a friend one evening, when all of a sudden firing started and his companion fell dead with a bullet through his forehead. Makinthan told me that he ran for his life leaving his friend where he had fallen.

The hardships of camp life meant that they had to survive for days on a ration of rice and lentils without any salt. Makinthan spoke of how they had no option but to use open fields for their daily ablutions even when women were around, "Vekkamey illaam'a..." – "Without shame..."

The rebels came to the camp one day and ordered Makinthan to join the fighting in spite of his mother's pleas that he was too young. He was taken away and sent into battle. He spoke of the terror of being at the forefront, not knowing when he would be hit by a bullet or captured. After a few weeks, he and a friend ran away from the army camp, helped by a kind-hearted older soldier, and they somehow found their way back to the refugee camp. Within a few weeks of their escape, the rebel army was defeated and the war ended.

Compared to what he had seen in his young life, I had lived a sheltered existence.

And so we struggled through the remainder of that year – somehow surviving through dreary lectures about parasites, viruses, and diseases, and what seemed like endless hours in the lab cutting into dead dogs, or looking at histopathology slides and bacterial cultures. Long hours were spent poring over the library's copies of past exam papers, trying to discern trends and strategise study plans.

Not a day went by without roundly cursing the rotten veterinary faculty canteen food and the hopelessly incompetent fellow who ran it– and yet, most days we ate there, since the other canteens on campus weren't exactly serving gourmet fare. And the food here was cheaper.

The only difference for me was that compared to the first year, now I had some company to share it all with.

One January morning, Makinthan and I were in the canteen taking advantage of a free hour to relax and have a cup of tea. I had spent the hour asking him about life in Jaffna and about places to see, telling myself for the umpteenth time that I would soon plan a trip up north. I wanted to see other parts of the island and the north sounded interesting.

Soon it was 10 AM and time for us to walk back to the class.

Makinthan returned our cups to the counter. Turning to me, he asked, "Bass, vareng'la?" – "Are you coming?"

"Enge?" I replied. "Where?"

The pinky finger came up again in the familiar gesture. "Urine pfass," he said.

"Okay," I said, standing up to join him.

What the hell.

—

By mid-May, we had finally crawled on all fours to the end of our fourth semester exams. We had been released from classes for three weeks of study holidays starting in the middle of March. With oceans of material, the days were spent in morning-to-night study, all the while knowing that we would never cover it all – especially given the sadistic mind-set of the powers-that-be in our department, who always scheduled theory exams one after the other, each day of the first exam week. This would be followed by practicals for all subjects spread out over the remaining four weeks.

By this time, I had long since abandoned any idealistic thoughts of immersing myself in my subjects and gaining the deep understanding that would make me that fantastic veterinarian – it was all about survival now. The best I could do was to look at exam papers from the previous years and get some sense of the pattern of questions. Study was done with the hope and a prayer that the examination would not drastically deviate from that pattern. Next, it was critical to have a plan – at least in my head – of what chapters I would try to revise on the evening before the exam. With this battle plan and some luck, I hoped to get that all-important C grade to pass.

"If you get anything above a C," I told myself, "take it as a bonus. But get that C."

Each subject had a laboratory exam as well as an oral one. Some like pathology had four practicals in total – the laboratory exam was split into two: gross pathology and histopathology. Then, we had something called a colour chrome exam, where the examiner displayed slides of about 30 different specimens on the projector and we had to answer questions on them, with two-and-a-half minutes for each slide. The final part was the viva voce.

In short, it had been a gruelling two months, and by the time we reached the end, all of us were ready to drop.

That evening, I decided to visit the hostel of the Jaffna boys and celebrate the end of our exams by having dinner with them. I caught a bus to their area and walked the last kilometre to their hostel, which was on the other side of the campus beside the Mahaweli river.

Makinthan was waiting for me, and as we walked to his room, he called Murugan on his mobile phone to inform him of my arrival. Murugan said he would come down to join us in Makinthan's room.

My first reaction upon entering Makinthan's room was one of shock. The room was tiny with barely any space to walk around the two cots and the two study tables. A tiny balcony had a small stove. Makinthan told me that whenever they decided to cook, they would do so in that balcony. At the end of the corridor was the common bathroom used by all the students in that wing.

The bedsheets hadn't been washed in years and the floor hadn't seen a broom probably since it was constructed. I couldn't understand how two students could live in that cramped, filthy space.

There was a knock on the door and in walked Murugan wearing a red t-shirt and a checked blue-and-beige lungi.

"Hello, Anand!" he greeted me enthusiastically. "First time in our hostel!!"

We settled down, Makinthan at one study table, and Murugan on the cot. I took the second chair by the study table.

The freedom from tension about the exams and the relief of not having anything to study meant that we were all in a sunny mood.

I had been in a different batch from the Jaffna boys and had been the last to finish the viva that day. The conversation naturally drifted towards the orals and I told them about the questions I had faced that day, the ones I had stumbled over, and which professor had been friendly and which one had asked the difficult questions.

As the evening wore on, the stories became more and more embellished, and our laughter, more and more raucous.

"My micro viva was a torture, machan." This was Makinthan.

"Did you fellows notice how Nachikesa sir, who is normally so friendly in class, was so stern in viva?"

"Yesss!" chorused Murugan and I.

"He asked me, what are the things you can do to confirm an E. coli infection in a farm. When I asked him: sir, are you referring to the biochemical tests, he just sat there looking at me, didn't say a word, machan."

"Nnooo!" I exclaimed in horror at this unspeakable meanness.

"My parasite viva was funny, machan," began Murugan, lounging on the cot and re-crossing his legs, while deftly manipulating his lungi.

"Daniel sir asked me to name the eye helminth of cattle. Confidently I answered Thelaria, machan. Then, he asked me how I could make a diagnosis... and like an idiot I said: by checking for eggs in the faeces! They both started laughing machan, saying "how can an eye worm appear in the faeces!!"

We all collapsed laughing.

"And guys, what was Jayakanthan sir doing at our micro viva? He never asked me any questions, just checked my record book and asked me to sign the register. Only the other two asked questions, Nachikesa sir and the lady from the research institute. Did he ask you fellows anything?" I asked.

"No," they both said. "His role was only to get our signatures…"

"Please sign here," said Murugan, mimicking our teacher and extending a sheet of paper.

"Ho ho ho ha ha ha," we all roared, at what felt to us that evening as the utter hilarity of a professor who never asked questions in a viva.

And thus I spent a pleasant evening in Makinthan's room.

Little did I know that that innocent visit to the hostel would expose me to another social peril.

By now it was close to 8 PM and we decided to step out to eat at a small restaurant which they told me served some decent fried rice and rotis.

First we went to Murugan's room because he wanted me to see it. It was a replica of Makinthan's room with the same two dirty-sheeted cots pushed up against one corner, and the two study tables and accompanying chairs.

"Who's your roomie?" I asked.

"Boopalan," replied Murugan.

I knew him – Boopalan was a friendly third year Tamil student. The Jaffna boys had introduced him to me once outside our faculty canteen. I remembered he had been very curious to know why I had chosen to study in Kandy.

"You both sleep on these cots?" I asked, still unable to digest the fact.

"Yes, me on this one, and that one is Boopalan's," said Murugan, pointing to the one against the wall. There wasn't even a one-centimetre gap between the two beds, so where was the question of 'that one is his, this one is mine,' I wondered to myself. Even dairy cows get a foot of head space at the feeding trough. This was terrible.

And just as I was grappling with the image of two students sleeping against one another, Murugan casually reached out for the clothes stand and picked up an underwear from the cluster of clothes lying on it.

I was paralysed with shock. All this time I had been chatting with a person who had had parts of his anatomy sashaying about all over the place... and during our chat in Makinthan's room, he had been twisting and turning on the bed with gay abandon. I guess growing up in Vavuniya makes you something of a free spirit.

He looked at it for a moment, no doubt doing a practised quality check. Suddenly he stooped to pull it on. Showing tremendous presence of mind, I put my head into the kitchen and pretended to be very interested in how they did their cooking.

Within seconds Murugan had pulled on his pants and we were ready to roll.

As we hit the road, Makinthan and Murugan walked ahead and I followed since there was no footpath and cars and buses were driving past.

"Without my lungi, it feels kind of odd," declared Murugan.

"Yes, only when I change into one as soon as I get home do I feel comfortable," agreed Makinthan.

And that was when Murugan dropped the grenade.

"All I know is that I wear it when I go to sleep. When I wake up in the morning, my lungi will be somewhere and I'll be somewhere. It's only the blanket that saves Boopalan!"

I stopped walking, thunderstruck by the horrifying images that flashed across my mind. But the Jaffna boys had already moved on to other topics and I hurried to keep up with them.

From that moment onwards, my respect for Boopalan shot to the stratosphere. A few days after my eventful visit to the hostel, I ran into Boopalan outside the canteen as usual.

Murugan's words and the image of the two cots next to each other flashed across my mind's eye again, as I walked up to Boopalan. The norm was to simply exchange verbal greetings, but this time, a simple "hello" just wouldn't do.

"Hello, Anand," he said. His smile turned to a look of surprise as I gripped his hand and put my feelings into it. "What's up?" he asked, and his face now began to look alarmed as I continued to hold his hand. "Nothing, nothing," I said, gathering myself and letting go. "I just wanted to say hi."

"I'm fine, you take care," he said as he backed away and I could see a quizzical frown where there had been a smile.

No doubt I had added some more fuel to the general impression about this crazy Indian who had quit his job to come and study veterinary medicine in Kandy. But it mattered not one bit to me. As far as I was concerned, Boopalan was the bravest man in the whole of Kandy and I just had to shake his hand.

Chapter Four

The Kennels

During my final year, the teaching hospital at my university was a bustling place that saw sixty to seventy cases on an average every day. We students were divided into five groups, with each group moving by rotation through the Out Patient Department (OPD), the intensive care unit (ICU), the Continuous Monitoring Unit (CMU), the pharmacy and the kennels.

The kennels were in a building to one side of the hospital and were quite basic in construction and facilities. Two rooms had a series of lengthwise enclosures, each about six feet by four feet in dimension with concrete floors and walls. Each kennel had a wire mesh door in front and each had a drain to wash away the mess if the wards urinated or defecated inside, which happened regularly and continuously. The house had a wall in the middle that divided it into two – one portion was the designated Isolation Ward that received patients with suspected infectious diseases, the most common one being puppies with parvoviral infections.

On the other side were non-infectious patients.

The kennel rotation was the most physically demanding rotation of all because it meant working outside in all weather conditions, walking back and forth multiple times between the hospital and the kennels. It also involved a lot of fetching, lifting and restraining of the patients from their enclosures. In addition, the patients had to be fed and walked.

Sadly, to me, it also felt that the kennels were where all the delinquents and discards of the animal world came. It was mostly filled with dogs – there was a separate cat ward in the hospital, so it was rare to see cats in the kennels. Of course, some of the kennel cases were awaiting surgery or recovering from it and were put there if there was no space in the recovery room. Others showed all signs of contagious diseases and it made sense to isolate them at least temporarily. But the kennels were equally full of the most heart-breaking cases – stray dogs that had been hit by a car or a train, dogs and cats with terminal illnesses, and several patients who didn't need to spend long lonely days shut up there with the smells, sounds and energy from a dozen other dogs to endure. Some of the dogs adapted well while others just couldn't handle it and would withdraw deep into themselves.

It was this last category of pedigreed, maladjusted dogs that distressed me the most. The strays seemed anyway moulded and cast in fires for having been born and bred on the streets where surviving each day was a triumph. They were there because some Good Samaritan had dropped them off after seeing them injured – many of them stayed on at the hospital grounds after recovery and joined the local pack.

The parvo and gastroenteritis pups were too young to really show any reaction to the kennels – if they were too sick, they became quiet and miserable due to the fever raging inside them and the diarrhoea leaking away all their energy. If they were generally of a sunny disposition and not too sick, they'd take their isolation without thinking about it – sleeping most of the time, wagging their tails when they saw a student and enjoying their short walks.

But the pets that came from homes were the most difficult to handle. Away from their families, they expressed their pain in different ways. The majority of them would show signs of depression, becoming quiet and sitting in a corner of their cages. Some became unnaturally aggressive. A few didn't show any ill effects and remained cheerful and active in spite of their stay in the kennels. There were some owners who cared about their pets and visited the kennels once, some of them twice a day, to talk to their pets and ask us how they were progressing. Many owners, however, never came, and these were the saddest cases, because it seemed like those dogs were unwanted and uncared for. They were left in the wards for weeks on end when they might have had a much quicker recovery at home, because the owner wanted to go on vacation, or didn't care enough to provide the pet with minimal care at home and would rather pay a hospital to do it.

It was in the kennels that I met three individuals who inspired, cheered and churned me.

The first one was a dog named Duke. and it was an apt name for what he must have once been – a beautiful black and tan German Shepherd in the prime of his life.

When I first got the case and saw him, I felt like I had been dropped into a deep ocean with a heavy stone tied to me.

He was recumbent on his left side on the floor of his kennel, staring straight ahead with an empty gaze at the concrete wall a few inches away. His coat, or what remained of it, was a dull matted mess with large pressure sores at his cheek bones, shoulder, and hip, showing how long he had been sick and unable to stand. He had stopped eating and drinking for several days, and although his coat still covered the worst of it, I was shocked when I placed a hand on his side – the ribs could hardly have felt more prominent on a skeleton. He had distemper with all the tell-tale, classic signs – the hyper-keratinised pads, the frequent paddling of the limbs, and the thick mucous discharges from the eyes that had crusted so that his eyes were half shut. And over everything was the smell – the stink of the diarrhoea that had pasted his rectum and soiled his tail and hind quarters, of the festering sores on his body, of the stale breath coming out of his mouth, the smell of impending death.

The clinician who was there gave me my instructions. "Poor dog," he said. "There is nothing much we can do for him other than supportive treatment. Try to keep him as comfortable as possible."

It was clear that he expected the patient to die soon.

"In such cases, isn't it better to euthanise the patient and put him out of this suffering?" I asked.

"Yes, we also recommended the same thing, but the owners aren't willing to let us put him down," came the answer.

And that was pretty much that. I squared my shoulders and took a deep breath before getting down to the task. Donning my gloves, I pushed my hands under Duke and lifted him onto the wooden tables placed outside to give medications to the kennel dogs. Down as he was to skin and bones, he couldn't have weighed more than fifteen kilogrammes.

The IV canula had already been placed in the cephalic vein of his foreleg. So I got the saline running and gave him his shots of antibiotic against secondary infections. I clipped the long, matted hair around the body sores, flipping him over to make sure the sores on both sides were covered. They had to be thoroughly washed out with saline and a diluted solution of povidone iodine. Finally, the wounds had to be wrapped in padding and bandage. The next task was to clean him up as best as I could. The perineal area had to be cleaned of the diarrhoeal remains and his eyes washed. I took a piece of cloth and soaked it in water before using it to give him a rub down.

The whole procedure had taken close to ninety minutes and I was tired and depressed at the end of it.

In my teens, one of my favourite authors had been James Herriot, the world famous and much-loved veterinarian from Yorkshire. His stories about patients that he had to euthanise came back to me. I remembered his words, about how he tried to talk to his patients and gently stroke them as he injected the overdose of the anaesthetic drug, so that as they faded away the last thing they would know and feel would be a gentle voice or a touch.

I decided I would adopt his method. As I placed Duke down back in his kennel and gave him some water in his mouth through a syringe, I stroked his head and ears and spoke to him for a minute. As I spoke his name, there was the slightest flicker of response in his eyes. "Good dog, Duke," I said. "Go in peace."

For the first time in my brief veterinary career, I prayed that the patient would die.

But it was not to be. Over the course of the next week to ten days, I had to repeat the same protocol morning and evening. I began to think of Duke as the dog that simply would not die. By day two, he had become so dehydrated in spite of the IV fluids that his veins had collapsed and inserting a new cannula became impossible. So, any fluids he was getting from that point on went in subcutaneously. He did not eat a morsel of food or drink any water other than what was forced down his throat.

Every day, I'd open the bandages to find that the sores had become just a bit worse than the day before, driving me to new depths of despair. And yet, Duke carried on, lying there, feet paddling, staring at the wall in front of him. Dying, but not going.

Each time, I'd say the same words. "Good dog, Duke. Nice dog. Go in peace."

Duke's family never came to see him. I wondered at this family that would not allow us to put him to sleep, but would also not come to visit. There was nothing we could do to save him and it would have been better for Duke to die in his home, rather than in a concrete cell. Surely, they must know that. Perhaps they could not bear to see him in this condition and could not provide the daily nursing care that we were giving him. It was not my place to judge. But one thing I knew: Duke needed them around him during these final days when he was suffering. I was a poor, poor substitute.

Duke took ten days to die. By that time, I had moved on to my next rotation, and my classmate who had taken over his case from me told me one morning that Duke had gone. I said a silent prayer for him, glad that his suffering had finally come to an end.

It was a case that swallowed me, twisted me around, digested a part of me, and then spat me out like a much chewed up paan. If only the owners had given Duke his standard vaccination shots when he was a puppy, he may have lived a full life. Why did the hospital agree to hospitalise Duke when there was clearly no chance of saving the patient's life? And if it did admit him, why was the owner's consent required for what was clearly a medical decision to alleviate suffering? As veterinarians, what were we genuinely able to do to save a life? Had we provided some comfort to that poor dog, or just prolonged his suffering before he finally passed on? All these questions ran round and round inside me and I had no answers.

—

Roxy was a growler. When I got the case, the others in the group told me to be careful because "she's a biter." I walked into the kennel to see this new patient, and there she was, sitting silently on one side of her cage, looking up sullenly at me.

At first sight, she looked like a Yorkshire terrier with the classic Yorkie moustache, the black and tan colouration, the hairy body and short tail. But Roxy's ears were strange-looking and she was a little too tall for a Yorkie. Roxy was a mutt. And she had attitude.

"Hi Roxyyy…" I called out before entering her enclosure.

"Grrrr… grrrr…" was her reply.

I tentatively held out my closed fist in front of her while looking a little to the side. I could feel her breath on my fist, but the growling emerging from the depths of her abdomen did not stop even for a second. Without making any sudden moves, I gently eased the chain off her neck, allowing her to get used to my presence. I moved about the kennel a little, then squatted down again beside my patient, looking at the hind legs that were spread out in a strange way. Gently, I ran my hand over Roxy's back, and while talking in a low voice to her, lifted her slowly to my side, to take her to the benches outside.

The growling abated a little and I soon realised that it was all an elaborate act. Roxy was harmless. Some dogs reacted to being in the kennel by barking madly when we worked with them. Others wagged their tails in joy at the human contact. Some of them would shrink in terror and some of them would take our prodding and handling with total equanimity.

Roxy expressed herself by growling. It wasn't even that she was irritated or scared. Whatever she was feeling, it was expressed the same way. When I greeted her and lifted her up in my arms, she would growl. When I jabbed her with a painful injection, she'd have that motorcycle engine gunning. If I fed her or rubbed her down, which was clearly a pleasurable experience, she'd still be growling non-stop. And the tone never varied. It was always the low pitched, continuous grrr… grrr... grrr...

At times I'd just laugh helplessly at her. The other students wouldn't handle her until they put a mouth gag on her for fear of being bitten. But I saw through her facade and never felt the need to use a gag, not even the first time. Once or twice she did snap at me, when she felt more pain than usual – it was just her way of telling me that she was hurting and that I needed to be more careful.

Roxy had somehow injured the lumbar area of her spine Her owner did not know how it had happened. When I palpated the vertebral column, I could not feel any clear fracture, but there was clearly some abnormality there. It felt more like an abnormal twist to the lumbar region than a fracture. Maybe she had wandered out of her house and some vehicle had hit her... or maybe she had got into a fight with a larger dog. Whatever the cause, the end result was that Roxy had lost control of her hind quarters. Her splayed hind legs dragged uselessly behind her, and she moved using only her forelegs. The injury had made her a paraplegic.

I had seen some terrible spinal injuries that had left dogs twisted out of shape, unable to move and in unbearable pain – Roxy was lucky. Her injuries seemed to be relatively minor because she didn't seem to be in pain except when some especially tender spots were pressed. She could move about on her own and generally seemed in good spirits.

But the lack of control over her rear end was a problem. As she moved around continuously dragging her hind legs behind, the spiral curls of her coat would get caked with dirt. Spinal injuries often result in damage to the nerves feeding the perineal region, which in turn leads to incontinence. But Roxy didn't seem to have that problem – an indication that the damage wasn't too severe. I fell into a routine with Roxy. Every morning, I would start with lifting her up on the workbenches and doing the general clinical examination. She would get her antibiotic shot if it was due. Then it would be time to clean her up and give her a quick rub down with the towel. Last of all came Roxy's favourite part – her morning and evening walks around the kennels.

I used a towel to support her hind legs for her daily walks. As I slipped the towel under her, she would sit impatiently waiting for me to start walking. Our conversation would go something like this:

"Ready for your walk, Roxy?"

"Grrr... grrr..."

"Okay, Roxy. Now go slow, otherwise the towel will slip and you'll tip over, okay?"

"Grrr... grrrr..."

"And there's no use running because I'm too tired to run, okay?"

"Grrr... grrr..."

It was the highlight of the day for Roxy. As soon as I stood lifting her hind quarters up with the towel, she would take off at a brisk trot – and here was a paraplegic dog that I struggled to keep up with. Any pain or discomfort was forgotten in the excitement of that daily walk. It was a relatively small area within the hospital grounds that we could walk the dogs in, but Roxy seemed to find new delights each time she walked. Every bush, every tree stump, had to be sniffed and investigated to make sure that nothing dramatic had changed in the few hours since she had last checked it.

I would take a break when we reached the grassy patch next to the surgery room – I don't know if she ever got tired but I usually was. It was the best time to give Roxy her physiotherapy massage after the warm up walk, especially if the sun was out. And so I'd lower the towel and squat down beside my patient.

As I stroked the head and ears, the motorcycle engine would start up again.

"Grrr... grrr..." Roxy would go.

"Oh, shut up, Roxy," I'd say as I stretched and massaged the hind legs and the pelvis.

"Grrr.... grrr…" she'd reply. And so it went on.

Slowly, ever so slowly, I began to see improvement. We used to let our patients sit out in the morning sun once their medications had been given and walks completed. It was good for them to interact with their fellow inmates and get some fresh air and sunshine before going back into their kennels.

Often, going off their food is the first sign that an animal is sick. They also become dull and lethargic, often shunning company and showing no interest in play or social interaction.

Roxy was eating and drinking just fine. She was bright and alert, and as soon as she was put down, she would take off on her two fore legs and keep going until she grew tired.

Once again, I had a case that would have done much better with home care.

All I was doing was giving Roxy antibiotic shots once in three days, cleaning her coat, and massaging her hind legs. It was up to nature to cure her. The same, or better level of care, could have easily been provided by her owner. In advanced countries I had heard of paraplegic animals being fitted with prosthetic devices, but such therapeutic aids had not yet reached Sri Lanka. Some students did try to make a wheelchair for Roxy using a broken pram and other odds and ends, but it didn't work and Roxy was not able to walk freely with it attached to her trunk. The contraption was quickly abandoned.

As I moved on from that kennel rotation, I felt that Roxy was definitely getting better. She really needed to be at home, not in the kennel.

With her zest for life and love for walking, the prognosis was bright. Even if she didn't get the full function of her hind limbs back, she'd be fine. All she needed was a wee bit of support and daily care from her family.

Roxy was going to growl her way through life just fine.

—

Desy's persona was such that she made her presence felt throughout the hospital, and her deep, booming bark would resonate all the way to the OPD. I heard her before I met her. And every student who handled Desy would talk about her to the others. She was just that kind of dog.

At first, I wondered if somebody had spelled her name wrong on the kennel board and if her real name was 'Daisy'. But no, I checked the file and her records and there it was – her name was 'Desy', not 'Daisy'. It's a phenomenon seen quite commonly in India and Sri Lanka where English is a foreign language and names get spelled phonetically.

Her file described Desy as being a German Shepherd, but some of her ancestors had surely carried on dalliances outside the clan because, although overall she could be described as German Shepherd-like, there were many features that showed her to have mixed ancestry. She was coal black from nose to tail and her coat – or what was left of it – hung from her body in thick, long strands. One thing was certain – Desy was a hound. I truly understood what the term 'loping' meant when I took Desy for her daily walk.

Other dogs walked. Desy loped. All those descriptions of 'loping hounds' came startlingly to life when I walked Desy. It is a gait that is difficult to describe... the first thing that struck me was how high Desy lifted her legs to take each step. While most dogs simply placed one foot in front of the other, Desy would lift each paw clear of the ground in a high arc before placing it down. Then there was the curious low-hung head position – as if she was reluctant to come too high off the ground level for fear of losing some important scent. The low head and high-stepping created an effect where her head would bob up and down in sync with each step. And she would pull on the leash with frenzied energy – "C'mon, c'mon," she was telling me, "Too many smells, not enough time!" I wish there was an open field where we could take her and let her loose – it would have been quite a beautiful sight, I'm sure, to see her run.

Demodicosis had left her looking bare and raw. Great patches of skin were left bald on Desy's body and her skin had become as thick as a rhino's hide. It was grey with angry wrinkles and sores all over, made worse by Desy's biting and scratching.

I took a skin scraping from one of the bare spots at the shoulder and looked at it under the microscope. There they were – a handful of the tell-tale cigar-shaped parasites that made diagnosis possible. Several types of fleas and mites feed on dogs and some, like Otodectus, Sarcoptes and Psoroptes look similar to me – like some weird repulsive creature imagined by a Hollywood studio for a Star Wars movie. Demodicosis or demodectic mange gets its name from the parasite Demodex canis that causes it. Mr. Demodex however, stands out in the crowd due to its distinct cigar shape. Even a novice like me could easily identify it. It's considered normal to find some Demodex mites on a pup, as they often get it from their mothers. It usually remains as a commensal on the skin, causing no clinical symptoms. But in times of stress or illness, when the immune system is below par, they can cause mange with a varying degree of symptoms. Looking at Desy's general joie de vivre, it was difficult to imagine stress being a trigger, but in reality, one never knows. Maybe she had got them from her mother or had been seriously sick, it was hard to know.

In any case, the treatment was relatively straightforward. Desy needed Ivermectin shots once in ten days and antibiotic cover for the sores and wounds on her body that were open invitations to bacteria.

To look at Desy was to have waves of distress wash over you. The large bald patches of grey, crusting, leathery skin, the cuts and the sores, and the bits of fur sticking on at odd places had turned Desy into an ugly dog. On top of that was the itching and burning that was causing her so much obvious discomfort. I couldn't handle her without my gloves. At first, I approached her with some trepidation and discomfort in touching her, more of my own making than anything else. Imagine my relief when I discovered that Desy was one of those beings that didn't care one bit about her appearance. She was a dog after all.

Desy craved only one thing in life. Attention.

She didn't care if that attention came in the form of painful injections or a nutcase in blue scrubs, with odd-smelling white hands pulling open her mouth, and inserting hard, pointed objects into her backside every day. As far as Desy was concerned, attention was attention. There was nothing good or bad about it.

She good-naturedly took her shots and would sit quietly as I cleaned her face and eyes. And she enjoyed her loping walks. There was, however, one added caveat in Desy's Laws of an Orderly

World: nobody was allowed to pay any attention whatsoever to other dogs when we were with her. After all, what did other dogs matter? She, the great Desy was there, right?

For me, this meant that I had to necessarily work with Desy last if I had other patients in the ward. But it wasn't just me. As my fellow students let the dogs out of their kennels and began working with their wards, she would explode into protest, barking non-stop in that deep booming voice that threatened to bring the hospital down.

One afternoon, I lost it. I was trying to give medications to a fractious patient – and here was this crazy dog barking as if the sky was falling on her head.

"HUSH, DESY, STOPPIT!" I yelled at the top of my voice. I fixed her with what I imagined to be a baleful glare.

"Woof, woof," went Desy, and I could see she was thrilled at this new game I had suddenly invented.

"SHUT UP!" I shouted, trying again.

"WOOF, WOOF!" Now Desy was really getting into mid-season form, bobbing up and down on her forelegs.

I quickly realised my stupidity: I was having a shouting match with a hound. And there was no way on heaven or earth that I could win that contest. Deflated, I gave up.

Abandoning my patient for the nonce, I went and sat down next to her.

"Wait Desy," I tried to cajole her. "I have to give medicines to your friend, you know that, right?"

In reply, I got a tail-wagging, adoring grin.

With hope in my heart, I went back to the other patient.

"Woof, woof," protested Desy behind me, not losing even an instant.

I gave up. I called one of my classmates over and asked him if he would take Desy for a walk while I finished up with my other patient. It was the only way to manage her, and everybody caring for Desy followed the same procedure – one student would walk Desy, while the others treated the kennel patients.

Desy's infection took about three weeks to clear up. Her hair started growing back and she no longer scratched and bit herself compulsively. The skin was also slowly returning to its normal, soft, white texture. On the day of her discharge, Desy got the bath of her life with about five students fussing over her, petting and scrubbing her, drying and combing her now-grown-back hair. Later, there was much competition as to who would take her on a walk. In the end, we compromised and two students at a time took her around the hospital block... this way, she got four walks. When her owners came to pick her up, we all crowded around Desy saying our goodbyes. The girls hugged her, while we boys gave her thumps on her back and petted her... and now nobody needed gloves. Everybody wanted a photo with her. Desy took it all in, wagging her tail non-stop, loping circles around our feet and grinning from ear to ear. She was loving every moment of it.

We were sorry to see her jump into the back of her owner's jeep. I suspect some tears were shed as the jeep pulled out of the hospital gates. I thought back to the times when we'd all be cupping our ears in despair when Desy was in one of her barking moods.

I thought back to the frayed nerves when my group discussed how to manage this patient. And yet, we would have all gladly gone through the whole process again, just for the sake of having that lovely, good natured, carefree-as-a-cloud dog in our midst.

That was Desy. She was just that kind of dog.

Chapter Five

Dairy Farms

As a veterinary student you get taken on a lot of field trips. If you're a student in Sri Lanka, then those field trips will be almost exclusively to dairy farms, as that is the most important industry in the country.

The compulsory field trips ("If you are absent, you will not be allowed to sit for the exam...") began in the first year and continued till the end of the course. It was the same drill each time – we students had to assemble at the crack of dawn at the faculty, since the farms were all hours away from the university. There would be a long, uncomfortable bus ride: and here, if you didn't have a gang of friends looking out for you to jump in early and 'book' a seat for you, you would spend a pleasant few hours standing in the bus aisle. I never did find out why the organisers couldn't make the simple connection that for the 80 odd students, two buses were needed for everyone to get a seat. Maybe it had something to do with the general attitude that places students somewhere between nematodes and poultry on the social scale.

And so, we would reach the farm after several hours and begin the tour. We would look at the housing for the cows, visit the calf barn, observe the milking, take notes about the feeding schedules and rations, and so on. There were some variations to the script – depending on the scale of the farm. It would either be a backyard operation, with the farmer himself mucking out the single barn and doing the feeding and taking his animals out to the field; or it would be a large commercial operation with hundreds of cows; with automatic milking machines in operation and tractors running through the barns and dropping rations in the feed troughs at feeding time.

There would then be a break for a packed lunch and then, after a short wrap-up discussion with the farm manager, we would start our long bus ride back. Whoever stood while coming would stand while going back too. It was the iron rule of dairy farm bus rides. The singing group complete with a tom-tom that had been in full action mode on the way up would now fall silent after a few desultory attempts at music – exhaustion would make half the batch fall asleep. It would usually be late in the night by the time we returned to Kandy.

It was only when we were in our third year that we saw stud bulls in these farms. After all the visits and seeing more dairy cows than I had thought was in my karma, coming upon a stud bull for the first time was a shock to the senses. The first thing that hits you when you see a stud bull is his sheer enormity. The bulls are like solid block mountains of muscle and attitude. They have a brooding presence and emanate a power that you see, that you feel, as you look upon them.

It was one of the intensive farms and this was their special barn for bulls. They had about half-a-dozen bulls of varying ages in that barn, and after I got over my initial shock, I walked up and down the aisle in a daze, unable to take my eyes off those magnificent beasts. I am just a shade under six feet in height, and I realised with awe that most of those bulls were as tall as me – at their shoulders. I walked over to look at the records chart that was posted on the wall – the average weight of those animals was one tonne.

Some of the older veterans simply stood at the back of their stalls and watched us as we walked past. No doubt they had had many gawking humans before us. Some, who seemed younger to my inexperienced eyes, reacted to our presence by stepping up and putting their faces over their pens to look at us. We could rub their foreheads safely from behind the protection of the concrete and iron gates. One of them repeatedly attacked the gate – which mercifully withstood the battering – making some students scream and run.

Once most of my batch had walked through the barn, I walked away from them to the far corner. A relatively quiet inmate came and stood next to the gate, allowing me to touch him. He stood silently there, and I observed him for a minute or so, looking in fresh disbelief at the expanse of his downturned neck. The dorsal side of his neck was as broad as two of me and was made of muscle and only muscle. I idly speculated as to what would happen if I had to carry out some routine procedure on such a patient and he took a sudden dislike to me.

Then, remembering that I was a veterinary student, I reached through the bars of the gate and began to feel his neck from the side, looking for the jugular furrow which is where vets locate the jugular vein to inject intravenous drugs or take samples of venous blood for testing. He was standing with his right side against the gate as still as a rock and something made me look up. What I saw in his face made me forget all about jugular veins and furrows. There was intense melancholy there and I felt like his eyes were trying to tell me about his sadness. Unlike his friend who was charging the gate, it seemed like he had fallen into a deep depression beyond any overt expression.

As I stood there with my palm on his neck, I considered his position. He had a fifteen feet square pen, and that was pretty much his world, except for the half-a-dozen occasions each year, when he would be required to mount the cows. Earlier, I had asked the manager whether the bulls were taken out to graze or if they had an open, more spacious enclosure. No, was the reply, because it became very difficult to handle them. Well, would you have a sunny disposition if you were put in solitary confinement all your life?

It was all terribly sad. The cows didn't exactly have a five-star life – after all, they were no more and no less than miniature milk factories themselves and nobody considered them as feeling beings. They were kept pregnant all their lives, separated from their calves soon upon or after birth, and milked literally for all they were worth, before being sent off to the slaughter house once their production of milk dropped below their maintenance cost. But at least they all lived together, were sent out to the fields, and had some semblance of a life. If you were unfortunate enough to be born male in the dairy farm world, one of two fates would befall you. One, you would be evaluated for breeding value. If you were of high pedigree, then it was a life of high energy concentrate feed, solitary confinement and the handful of planned outings every year, when you had to perform your duty and mate with all the cows in heat presented to you. This was until fresher studs would replace you – and then, of course, you were sent off with a one-way ticket to go under the knife. If you were found to be of poor genetic value, you would be collected soon after birth, put in a van with your male cousins and sent off to the slaughter house.

To me, the fate of the second group was preferable. At least their life of suffering was brief, even if full of terror and pain.

I wanted to tell that bull how sorry I felt, but somehow, no words came. In any case, no matter what I said, it would have been so trite. To condemn such a majestic animal to a life in a tiny pen is a travesty, a sadness that no words can capture. I joined veterinary school because I wanted to heal animals, to relieve them of pain and suffering. But here was a specialisation within my chosen profession, where the vet's job was to keep animals healthy so that they could continue their life of suffering.

I felt a great heaviness inside as I left the farm and boarded the bus. This time, there was no internal carping about having to stand for long hours. After all, once I got back home, I could stretch out and sleep, forgetting all about the prison I had seen that day.

Chapter Six

Summer at Patuxent

In the summer following my third year, I thought I'd go to the U.S. to work at a veterinary hospital and get some training. I had fond memories of volunteering experiences at animal hospitals there when I had lived there earlier as a graduate student. I thought it would be fun to go back as a vet student and work at a vet hospital again.

I knew the process would take time, so I started writing to hospitals in the U.S. about their following year's summer externship programmes in July itself. I thought it would be a fairly easy application process. After all, these were volunteer positions and I had many years of experience. As it turned out, externship positions at U.S. veterinary hospitals were much sought after by U.S. veterinary students and I received scores of rejections before finally landing an externship.

I had to get approval from my faculty to travel during my summer break for this adventure. The norm at my vet school was that in the summer break between the third year and the final year, students would be assigned to various farms around the country for what they called 'industry-based training'. I had to convince my faculty that I wanted to do my training in the U.S.

As with everything in Sri Lanka, getting approval from the faculty board was like fighting uphill through waist-deep snow with an avalanche bearing down upon you. The first step was to speak to the lecturer who was in charge of the summer industrial training programme. After hearing me out, he assured me that he would raise the subject at the next faculty board meeting scheduled for a date in October and that he would try to push through approval for my request.

I made sure I reminded him about my request whenever I ran into him in the intervening months.

Whenever I wrote to a hospital and requested a spot in their externship programme, their first question was always, 'What dates are you planning to be here?' to which I had no reliable answer because, for one, our exam and vacation dates were not out, and secondly, I still didn't know if the faculty would approve my plans. Added to this was the fact that the longer I waited to book my air tickets, the more difficult and expensive it was going to get.

The next time I met the lecturer was sometime in late October. When I reminded him about my request, he casually informed me that he had forgotten to bring up the topic. "When is the next board meeting?" I asked him. "Not sure," was his reply.

On such occasions, keeping an expressionless face and staying polite was a real challenge. But eventually, the next board meeting rolled up, and this time, he did bring up the possibility of my travel to the U.S. for my industrial training. I finally heard in March that the board had tentatively approved my plan.

During all this time, the nerve-wracking applications to hospitals had continued apace. Ten days before the start of my third-year exams, I received an email from the Patuxent Wildlife Research Center accepting me as an extern.

And so, from the middle of April to the end of May in the year 2016, I went to the Patuxent Wildlife Research Center (PWRC), now known as the Eastern Ecological Science Center, at Laurel, Maryland, on the upper eastern shore of the U.S. Although it was already summer in Sri Lanka when I reached there, winter was just sliding into spring in America. In my first two weeks at PWRC, I witnessed a spectacular transformation – the wildlife refuge is spread over a verdant 100 acres of undulating land and covered in trees. In the beginning, the trees still had their winter clothes on, which of course meant that they were almost naked, with only a few dying leaves clinging on to their bare greyness. Almost before my eyes, they became covered in an explosion of leaves, so that while earlier I could see for hundreds of metres through the forest, now a curtain of green reduced visibility to a few metres.

That was the other thing – they seemed to sprout leaves almost down to the ground. The wildlife refuge turned into a softly beautiful land of shimmering, sensual greenness. I never tired of driving through the winding roads of those forests to the different pens that housed our patients.

My five weeks at PWRC turned out to be an immersion in avian medicine. The wildlife refuge was at the heart of a 40-year-old collaborative effort to save the whooping crane, an endangered species that now survived only in pockets in Wisconsin, Louisiana, and Florida, with a migrant population in Canada. A captive colony of some 130-140 whooping cranes was maintained at PWRC and was their main work. In addition, there were colonies of sandhill cranes, kestrels, screeching owls, and several species of wild ducks like surf scoters, white winged scoters, wood ducks and black ducks.

I met one of the whoopers on my very first day. My mentor and trainer at PWRC, was their head veterinarian, Dr. Glenn Olsen, who had decades of experience in treating wild birds and was a veteran of the whooping crane programme. Whooping cranes had been driven close to extinction and this programme was started in 1966 to raise a captive-bred population of cranes and release them back into the wild.

We drove over to the whooping crane pens to do a physical on one citizen. PWRC had a platoon of wildlife technicians who were experts in handling and restraining cranes. I watched the whole operation from a safe point outside the wire mesh of the pen.

The technician picked up a broom and stepped up to the door of the pen. As soon as she stepped in, she shut the door as the whooper came at her. To my surprise, the technician stuck out her gum booted foot, and the whooper obligingly attacked it, pecking at the sole of the boot with impressive vigour. Once the crane slowed down, she next pushed it back with her broom, and then in one quick move, stepped up to the side of the bird, grabbed it around its middle and clamped down on its wings. She held the crane so that its head was pointing backwards and its legs were restrained and presented to the front. Now the vets could do their physical examination of the crane.

Dr. Olsen showed me the method to do a physical on a bird after first handing me a pair of plastic transparent goggles for protection. Even when it is under restraint, the crane has its neck and head free and it will peck at your eyes.

The crane got a shot of Ivermectin into its breast muscle and then came the fun part. She had to get her de-worming medicine, and this had to be given orally, using an oesophageal tube. Under Dr. Olsen's direction, I took the tube, opened up the crane's mouth and gently inserted the tube down the oesophagus, which was visible as two openings on either side of the trachea. I placed my fingers on the crane's neck and felt the tube go down, and then injected the dose of Panacur in.

And that was it – since the cranes have such long, thin necks, you can actually see and feel the tube as it slides down next to the trachea. Such are the simple joys of veterinary practice.

On my second day, I was joined by another veterinary student. Cooper was from the University of Wisconsin veterinary school and was getting ready to graduate. Unlike me who had just finished my third year, he was ready to enter the big scary world of professional veterinary medicine, and this was his last externship rotation before he started interviewing for jobs. Cooper and I forged a good friendship and worked well as a team in those two weeks that he was there. As my senior, I often depended on him to lend a helping hand when I was stuck on a task.

He had a quirky, yet charming way of expressing his satisfaction whenever he felt a job had been well done. I first noticed it when we brought out a hospitalised patient, a surf scoter, who had somehow managed to cut her leg on the wire mesh of her pen, and that needed a fresh dressing.

I brought out the duck and placed her on the examination table. I restrained her while Cooper removed the old dressing, cleaned out the cut and dabbed on some triple antibiotic before placing a new piece of cotton and finishing the dressing with gauze and plaster. I thought it was very professionally done and resolved to learn how to do dressings like that before I was finished at PWRC.

"Ta-daa!" went Cooper in a sing-song tone as he stepped back and critically examined his work. "That's done," he declared.

Over the fortnight that followed, I heard that expression several times. When we had finished the tedious job of processing blood and faecal samples, Cooper would express his relief with a "Ta-daa!" Or when we had finished a batch of vaccination shots for the duck colony, again, he'd go "Ta-daa!"

Once we had just finished the day's work and put away all the instruments and folders in the lab, and that was enough to make Cooper break out into a "Ta-daa!" He was just a happy vet, was Cooper.

—

One of the projects that we did at PWRC was analysing the blood of their captive sea duck colonies using a portable blood analyser machine called an i-STAT. It looked similar to one of those credit card machines you see at supermarket counters, except that it was somewhat larger in size and white in colour, with more buttons on the surface and a slot to print out the results on a small sheet of paper roll.

Instead of the hours that it would take a lab to process a blood sample, this device gave results in minutes. It had slots to put your blood sample in and insert a cartridge; and then all you had to do was enter your batch number, specify what kind of blood analysis you wanted and hit the enter button. i-STAT would do the rest and spit out the result. I could see how it could be hugely practical and useful, especially while working in field conditions.

But in order for it to work, you needed a sample of blood from your subject. And therein lay my challenge. Venipuncture in dogs and cats itself is hard, but taking blood from the jugular veins of ducks using a syringe and needle took the degree of difficulty to a whole different level.

For starters, the jugular vein on ducks is extremely small – at least in dogs and cats, once the fur has been shaved and the vein arrested, it pops up fairly clearly due to the pressure. In ducks, any sighting of the vein seemed to be more of a mental visualisation process rather than an actual sighting.

Secondly, it requires a serious level of skill and dexterity, because unlike in larger animals, you cannot really have one person arresting the vein while you employ both your hands and concentrate on extracting blood. With ducks, you need one person to restrain the duck and hold its head and neck in a stretched position. You then use one hand to arrest the vein while using your other hand to both insert the needle and withdraw blood in one smooth motion. It helps if you have long fingers, as you use your forefinger and thumb to insert, while pulling back with your ring and pinky fingers.

The neck is covered in feathers – in the case of the scoters and black ducks that we were working with, these were dark brown or black feathers. Even after smoothing down the feathers with alcohol, it was quite impossible for a novice like me to see anything that seemed remotely like a tiny corded rope running along the neck, which would have been the jugular. From theory, I knew where the jugular was supposed to be. I knew it was there... I just couldn't see it, never mind hit it with my needle.

Dr. Olsen tried his best to train me on the correct technique. He showed me how to arrest the jugular vein just above the thoracic inlet, then insert the needle and draw back on the plunger. The first time I tried it was on a white-winged scoter – and now I believe in such a thing called Beginner's Luck – because I hit the vein immediately.

"All right," said Dr. Olsen. "Woo-hoo," said Betty, the duck facility manager, who held the duck expertly while we drew blood.

"Well, this is easy enough," I thought foolishly to myself, wondering what all the fuss was about.

I found out in the next few minutes... and hours... and days. Because after that first duck, try as I might, I just could not draw blood from a duck. We went back to the duck pens on a handful of occasions during the next week, drawing samples from as many ducks as possible.

Cooper was good at it and rarely missed getting blood from his ducks. Only once or twice did I see him give up and call Dr. Olsen for help. There were a few times when Dr. Olsen himself missed hitting the vein, and he'd say in a mystified tone, "Even I'm having trouble hitting the vein today…"

But that was poor solace for me, as I became increasingly nervous around the ducks. To my harried mind, the silly birds seemed to struggle and thrash about just that bit more when it was my turn to work on them.

I convinced myself on several occasions that my needle was just about to get the vein when the duck made a sudden jerk and pushed the needle out. In reality, the poor ducks were probably sick and tired of this incompetent buffoon who kept jabbing and poking about their necks and were making their feelings known.

The sorry scene played out repeatedly at the duck pens during that week. Betty and her crew would haul in the ducks in their boxes, then bring them out one at a time. They would call out their identity tag numbers so that Carla the veterinary technician could start entering the data on the sheets. Next, the bird would be weighed and Cooper and I would take turns to do quick physicals and give them their West Nile virus vaccination shots.

Now the scene was set to draw blood.

Up I would step to my bird.

Dr. Olsen would hover behind me each time I attempted to draw blood, murmuring encouragement, or pointing out a mistake.

Willing myself to stay still, I would breathe (I thought) evenly and deeply while pouring some alcohol on the neck of the poor duck. Next, I would pinch down on the trachea at the point where it joins the shoulder, to clamp down on the jugular vein.

I would then make my first attempt by pushing the needle in where I thought the vein ought to be. Pulling back on the plunger, I would wait for the blood to come into the syringe.

Nothing.

I would then draw out the needle and try again. This time, I'd get blood all right, but instead of the syringe, it would collect in a spreading pool on the bird's neck feathers.

"You went through it," would be Dr. Olsen's comment.

"Ta-daa!" That came from somewhere behind me, signalling another home run for Cooper.

By now I'd be sweating and breathing heavily, as I withdrew the needle and made a third attempt. To my alarm, there would still be no blood, but now a new development – a small bump would appear on the bird's neck.

"Now you've got a haematoma," Dr. Olsen would say.

"Ta-daa," the sing-song victory cry would be heard again.

"Okay, you can try one more time, then I'd better take over," Dr. Olsen would say finally. "Three strikes and you're out... The duck is pretty stressed out."

Well, that was a moot point. Whose nerves were more frayed by that time, the bird's or Anand's?

Once more I'd apply the alcohol and clamp down on the neck. "I can see it!" I would hear Dr. Olsen exclaim.

He must have had X-Ray vision, because I could see sweet nothing.

Again, I'd try and again I'd come up with nothing. Shoulders slumped, I'd hand the apparatus to Dr. Olsen.

He would step up, and with nonchalant ease, insert the needle. As he drew back on the plunger, the syringe would fill with a spurt of blood.

"I don't know what else to tell you," he'd say, "You're doing everything correctly, but it's practice. It's just practice."

"Ta-daa," would come the by now familiar background music from my friend. Well, at least one of us knew what he was doing out there.

—

Dr. Olsen came to my help. "First," he said, "you need to develop the dexterity to insert the needle and pull back at the same time, without moving the needle. You are moving your hand too much. Go home and practise on a fruit."

So that was my first task. I did as he told me. I took a 3 cc syringe and a 25 gauge needle with me home and found an apple that would be my subject. And I practised the motions of withdrawing blood on it again and again, until I began to feel that I could do it automatically without having to remind myself of the steps.

There was, of course, no tiny vein to try and get into on the apple, nor did it twist and thrash about as I was doing the procedure. But still, it helped to get my hands used to the feel of inserting the needle and withdrawing the plunger in one smooth action. The apple became shrivelled and sad, but I poked and drew, poked and drew until I had the motion down.

The next stage in my graduation to my yellow belt in the venipuncture of ducks was to actually do it on live birds. Dr. Olsen sent me and Cooper to the duck pens one afternoon to practise and instructed Betty and her crew to give us American Black Ducks. Black Ducks were the largest of the duck species in captivity and so, naturally, had larger jugulars compared to the scoters and wood ducks.

Maybe because I knew this was only practice, or the fact that I had been working that apple over, I felt pretty relaxed going in for that afternoon session of duck-puncturing.

We started on the ducks and Cooper, after hitting the jugular dead centre on his first three ducks, declared that he was happy with his practice. He devoted the rest of the afternoon to helping me.

By this time, I had also tried three ducks and had drawn three blanks. Curiously, I still felt calm and relaxed.

"Cooper, can you actually see the vein?" I asked.

"No," he said to my great relief. "What I do is to start at the neck muscles, because I know that the jugular runs just a bit below them. I visualise where the vein might be, and then try to insert the needle into the middle of that spot."

"You have to figure out what method works for you," said my friend. "Because everyone has got their own way of doing it... I also find it useful to use my thumb to position the needle at the proper angle."

He indicated how he balanced the needle on the thumb of his left hand that was arresting the vein.

"Try pulling back on the plunger a bit as soon as you go in," said Betty, who was helping with restraining the birds. "Sometimes even if you don't hit the vein immediately, you just need to move it a bit and you get it."

I tried to follow those tips. Pressing the trachea down with my left hand, I felt with my right one for the neck muscles. I tried to imagine where the jugular might be running just below those muscles. And then, I slowly inserted the needle into the middle of my spot and withdrew the plunger at the same time.

A lovely crimson stream of blood jetted into the syringe. "There you go!" exclaimed Cooper and I was thrilled and relieved in equal measure. I collected about one cc of blood and Betty had the second duck ready for me.

Following the same method, I inserted the needle and pulled back on the plunger. Again, the beautiful spurting red fluid gushed in from the duck's jugular into my syringe. I was on a roll.

As I started on my third duck, I think I actually believed that I would hit the jugular vein again. Again, I inserted the needle just below the neck muscles and pulled back. And again, the syringe filled with blood.

"Ta-daa," said Cooper, as if he'd expected nothing less from me from the very start.

"Woo-hoo!" whooped Betty. I grinned delightedly at them.

"Okay, Anand, you'd better quit while you're ahead," said Betty. "When I was learning how to do this, I hit a few veins and felt good... and then when I kept going, I missed a few… I ended up walking away all sad that day."

I thought that was sage advice, so I took it. We packed up. Cooper and I walked back to the hospital to report my success.

In the end, I cannot say with conviction that I will get the jugular when I try it next. But I think I will know the right method and will be able to work out what to do if I'm missing them. It's a combination of skill, staying still, and being relaxed.

Dr. Olsen was right. It's practice. Just practice.

—

The five weeks at Patuxent went by in a flash.

One day during my last week at Patuxent, a female kestrel was brought in at the hospital with a rectal prolapse. About five inches of her innards were hanging out of her backside.

With rectal prolapses, the veterinarian's first approach is to push the organ back into place. Dr Olsen instructed us to wash the tissue with Lactated Ringer's Solution, after which he tried to push it back through the anus. We had no luck and the tissue kept popping out again.

There was no option left but to go in for surgery. The kestrel was given general anaesthesia and she was asleep in minutes. The anaesthetic causes relaxation of the muscles, so that this time, when Dr Olsen pushed the rectal tissue through the anal orifice, it went in smoothly. He then daubed Betadine on the site to prevent any infection and we gave her a subcutaneous saline injection for hydration as she was mildly dehydrated.

Dr Olsen applied a purse string suture, and the job was done. The kestrel looked as good as new. The whole operation had taken about fifteen minutes.

Disaster struck the next day. I reached the hospital at about 7.30 AM. The team was at the crane chick building, so the hospital was empty. Thinking I'd take a look at our kestrel patient to see how she was doing, I went to the recovery room. I knew immediately that all was not well as the kestrel was standing at a corner of its cage facing the wall like a child who had been punished.

When animals are healthy, they are alert, and especially so around humans. Mentation is a factor that vets look for while assessing general health – this bird's mentation was all wrong and she was apathetic and depressed.

I thought I'd flag Dr Olsen about it once they were back and left it there. However, half an hour later when I checked again, the situation had worsened. The kestrel was now recumbent on the floor of her cage and unresponsive to my touch.

Panicking now, I started calling the mobile numbers of the team – they walked in as I was calling and we placed the listless kestrel on the examination table.

The first thing to do was to check the sutures – they were intact and there was no swelling or discharge from the area, so that looked all right.

"I'll have to open the stitches," said Dr Olsen to Cooper and me. "Why don't you both do a quick physical while I get ready?" he suggested as he washed his hands and pulled on the gloves.

Cooper and I started the physical, when we felt the kestrel go very still.

"I think she just died, Dr Olsen," said Cooper, putting his stethoscope in his ears. With a grim expression he listened to a heart that had by then stopped forever. The kestrel had died on the table even as we were trying to understand what was wrong with her.

There was nothing much left to do except open her up to see what had caused the death. Necropsies are never great fun for me – working on dead bodies cannot be – but this was even more depressing than usual. When Cooper and I opened up the abdominal cavity, it revealed mustard coloured ovaries and fluid all over the peritoneal cavity.

"Well, there you go," said Dr Olsen, when he came over to check what we had found. "She had egg yolk peritonitis."

I found it hard to feel any satisfaction at having found the cause of death; or the fact that the prolapse had nothing to do with her death. All I could think of was that yesterday, we were sitting in quiet triumph at what seemed like a successful surgery. Today, she was dead.

—

On my last day at Patuxent, I decided to take a walk from the hospital to the crane pens. As I stepped on the winding road, I listened one more time to the swishing of the trees in the breeze as they butted heads over the road. I had walked about a hundred metres when a box turtle stepped out of the forest and started crossing. I stopped so as not to alarm the turtle and waited until it had almost crossed over before commencing my walk again.

I soon reached the crane pens and stood outside the fence, admiring their grace and beauty as they walked around. Compared to 40 years ago, when they were on the brink of extinction, things were looking up... with such a conservation project dedicated to saving them, I felt hopeful about their future. Whooping crane pairs often call out to each other as they forage, and when one crane calls out to its mate, the answer comes in a characteristic one-two return call.

It was time to say goodbye. I was by now familiar with their calls, so on an impulse, I called out to the crane closest to me: "Whoop!" and waited a few moments. The crane stopped his search in the grass for food and stood up. Throwing back his head, he let out an answering call. "Whoop! Whoop!!"

PART 2

Lost & Found in Sri Lanka

CHAPTER SEVEN

The Charm of Living in Sri Lanka

Being a veterinary student in Sri Lanka meant that I was living life in the trenches, so to speak – and that exposed me to some quirks of life there.

Just around the corner from where I lived was a neighbourhood kiosk that sold tea, the ubiquitous vaddes, buns, coconuts and bananas. I had often seen a gaggle of men sitting there in the evenings, chatting and drinking tea, or eating a snack. It was like a meeting point for all the rickshaw drivers, the local mechanic and sundry other workers. As was very common in Sri Lanka, the owner's house was behind the shop – or rather, the shop was simply the front portion of his house.

The owner was probably about forty or forty-five years old and he was the epitome of what is generally known as a 'sunny personality'. He would open his shop for business by 6 AM, putting up the boards only at around 10 PM. Every time I passed, he would wave at me with a broad smile and call out a hello in greeting.

I also noticed that he regularly fed the street dogs and cats as well as crows of the area. There was a sort of broken tree stump across the road from his shop and he would leave leftover food on it for his friends. For that reason alone, I would have wanted to be his regular customer.

There was only one problem. He had absolutely no concept of personal hygiene.

I once noticed while chatting with him, that his palms were covered in a fine sheen of black. Maybe it was from handling the wood stove in his kitchen, I don't know. But the hands were always like that... in fact there was a general air of blackness about him. Literally speaking that is; as if all his edges were tinged with soot...it was probably my overactive imagination.

I told myself that I couldn't be so fussy. After all, all those other people were regulars at his place, so it couldn't be that bad. And at least when he served me, he used tongs to pick up the buns or other items I purchased.

And so, one lovely sunny October Sunday morning, just after my fifth semester exams were over, I decided that I would purchase my breakfast buns from him that day, instead of the bakers where I regularly shopped. Bending to avoid my head bumping into the low roof at the entrance, I walked in.

Out he came.

"Hello, good morning!" he boomed. Oh, that brilliant grin and the happiness on his face: it was as if all the planets had come into alignment because Anand had chosen to visit his shop that day.

"Good morning," I replied, smiling back.

"Can I have one of that, and that?" I asked, pointing at two buns.

Scratch, scratch, he went, his hand on his head.

"Yes," he nodded vigorously, holding up his hand. He didn't speak English, and my Sinhala was still hopeless, so our communication was mostly through monosyllables and hand signals.

He went in and returned with a paper bag.

Picking out the buns with the tongs, he dropped them into the bag. Then handing it to me, he stood there happily.

Scratch, scratch. His armpit this time.

I was unfazed. I decided that it would be a good idea to buy a banana as well for lunch. He usually kept his bananas on a stand outside his shop, so I stepped back out. There were only two sad looking specimens there.

"No more bananas?" I asked him, pointing.

"Wait," he said, going inside one more time. He came out holding a nice big banana and he handed it to me with pride.

"40 rupees," he declared.

Scratch, scratch. This time he was pulling at his nether regions.

I paid and left saying my goodbyes. Well, what was the harm? He had not touched the buns directly while putting them into the bag. And the banana was completely safe. I would after all be peeling it and only eating the inside part.

—

Asking for directions in Kandy can be a hazardous business. I first experienced this in the early months after moving there, when I was searching for a place to stay.

It took me a few attempts and many miles of hiking the up-and-down streets of Kandy before I understood the 500 Metre Hoax.

This is how my direction-seeking scenes usually played out: I would show a passer-by an address I had written down and ask him, "Can you tell me how to reach this address?"

"Yes, go to that turning," he would say, pointing, "and it's 500 metres away on the right side."

Relieved at getting such clear directions, I would thank him and start walking.

And keep walking.

Twenty minutes later, I would stop another kindly looking gentleman (in Kandy, if you're male, you don't ask women on the road random things). Showing him my scrap of paper with the address again, I would ask him if he could help.

"Yes, yes," he would reply thoughtfully. "You have passed it... walk back 500 metres and you'll see a small side street. It's there."

With time, I understood that to a Kandyan on the street, distances, like life itself, are all relative. No matter where you're going, it's 500 metres away.

Not multiples or fractions of 500 metres. 500 metres.

I soon started taking auto-rickshaws to cover those 500 metre distances when going to look at rental houses.

At one point, being on the verge of a nervous breakdown, I thought I would ask for directions to the moon, just for fun. But I could guess the answer I would get, "Take a three-wheeler to such-and-such a junction. Get off, then walk 500 metres up the hill. Moon is there."

Two years into my adventure in Sri Lanka, I was once walking to the market to buy my monthly ration of sugar and biscuits. The supermarket was on a big main road that led to a roundabout at one end, with banks, the main court house and shops along its length.

Two gentlemen approached me and asked me something in Sinhala – the words 'BOC Bank' caught my ear and it wasn't too hard to understand that they were asking me where the Bank of Ceylon was.

"Yes," I replied, turning around and pointing down the road towards the roundabout. "500 metres," I said. "On this side," I said, waving my left arm about to show them that they didn't need to cross the road.

Nodding their thanks somewhat doubtfully, they walked on. I'm sure they double-checked with someone else, because I had a completely inappropriate grin on my face as I gave them the directions. But irony aside, my directions were accurate: the Bank of Ceylon really was half-a-kilometre along the same road, on the left side.

—

The same Bank of Ceylon ATM was the one from which I used to regularly withdraw cash for day-to-day expenses. The main road had a small water body running alongside it. It was one of my little pleasures to take walks along its banks in the evenings. I say 'water body', because it would change character from time-to-time. On days when people had dumped more than the usual trash into it, it was no more than a sewer. On days of heavy rainfall, it became – to my imagination, at any rate – a raging coffee-coloured Amazon. During the beautiful summer days, it was a quiet brook, with lapwings working its banks and swifts flitting about.

So, on days when I remembered that my cash balance was getting low, I would stop at the Bank of Ceylon on these walks to take out some cash. One evening, when I walked over to the ATM, there was a person inside withdrawing cash. There was also a Maruti car parked near the ATM and a man hanging about between the car and the ATM. I wasn't sure if he had come to take out cash, or was just admiring the impressive frontage of the bank, so I asked politely, "Excuse me, are you in the queue?"

For a second, he was thrown off, as people usually are in Kandy public life, when somebody addresses them in English.

Recovering and shaking his head vigorously, he said, "No problem."

Based on my life experiences up to that point, I took his answer to mean that he wasn't in the queue and that I could step up to the ATM next. But the reality was different.

Upon giving me that cryptic response, he moved imperceptibly closer to the ATM, making sure at the same time that he blocked my path to it. It was like he was at the starter's line, waiting for the start gun to go off. Sure enough, as soon as the user stepped out of the ATM, he was inside in a flash.

I was left to ponder over the vagaries of language and communication as I awaited my turn.

—

The most bizarre experience while asking for directions happened in Colombo. I was once there to apply for an extension of my visa – an annual torture that I had to endure since the Sri Lankan immigration department, with all its inscrutable sagacity, refused to give me a visa for the full duration of my veterinary course.

I was staying at a dorm in the area known as Slave Island and decided to go for a walk in the evening. Downtown Colombo has an old hospital that was built during Dutch rule, which has now been converted into a shopping centre. It's called the Dutch Hospital and is usually full of activity in the evenings. So I decided that I would try to find my way there.

I had a vague idea about the direction in which it lay. Accordingly, I started walking. At one point, while waiting to cross a wide bustling road at the zebra crossing, I thought I would just check if I was heading in the right direction. There was a local next to me also waiting to cross – from his white shirt, black trousers and formal shoes, I deduced that he was an office-goer, heading back home after a day's work.

"Excuse me," I said. "Is this the right road to Dutch Hospital?"

"Yes, just keep walking along this road," he replied, as we started crossing the road.

The conversation continued as we were crossing.

"Where are you from?"

"India," I said, looking left and right, the way my teachers in nursery school had taught me, to avoid being run over.

"Are you on Facebook?" he asked, when we reached the middle divider of the road.

"Wha... what?" I managed.

"Facebook," he repeated.

"Yes," I replied hesitantly, wondering where this was going, while trying my best to reach the other side of the road safely.

"What's your Facebook ID?" he asked, whipping out his cell phone.

We had, by this point, thankfully crossed without mishap.

"Anand K," I replied.

"Okay, I'll send you an invite," he replied cheerfully. And with a wave, he went on his way.

I suppose I could have lied and given him some false ID. But how pathetic would that have been? To lie to a person I'd just met 15 seconds ago... and that too about something as utterly absurd as my Facebook profile?

Once I got over the surreal experience, I chuckled to myself all the way to the Dutch Hospital. I don't know of any other place in the world where the price of getting directions is to be connected forever in cyberspace.

Chapter Eight

Pigs or Poultry, Horses or Cows?

In the beginning, all animals fascinated me and I wanted to minister to them all. It's true that all animals are wonderful, each species, in its own way. But being a vet to all animals is really not the same thing.

And so, as I progressed through the gruelling years of my course, I found myself knocking off options, one by one. The first to go was poultry medicine. Individuals sometimes brought their pet chickens to the farm for treatment, and it was charming to see how much those owners loved their birds. It was no different from pet owners who came to the small animal hospital with their cats and dogs, except that the pet in these cases was a rooster.

However, most of our work was with commercial poultry farms, which had thousands of birds being raised for eggs or meat. The nature of veterinary work changes when there are such large numbers and when the birds are not pets, but economic units. The focus then changes from the individual "My hen is not eating like normal," or "There is some growth on my bird's foot," to disease outbreaks that could affect the flock as a whole and cause economic loss to the farmer.

Then, the complaint is usually along the lines of "…ten of my flock have died over the past week," because it is often mortality that alerts the poultry farmer that something is amiss. Decisions are driven by economics.

Visits to poultry farms always left me feeling listless and heavy. Whether it was a layer farm producing eggs, or a broiler farm for meat, the setting was the same. The pens were large sprawling houses that would quite literally be jam-packed with chickens jostling for space. The sole mission of a broiler farm is to get the chickens as large and fat as possible in the 42-day period from their birth to slaughter. The result is that you see cases of heat stress and breast sores, where the chickens become so fat that their legs cannot support them and they drag their breasts on the floor. Layer birds are usually kept for a period of one-and-a-half years before their natural productivity starts dropping and they are culled for meat. Luckily, our teaching farm did not employ the battery cage method of raising layers, where the birds spend their entire lives inside cages so small that they can't even turn around. To me, that is even more cruel than packing 10,000 chickens into a pen and fattening them up for slaughter.

It didn't take long for me to understand that poultry medicine really wasn't my scene. Any lingering doubt was effectively blown away and buried forever on the day I had to de-beak a chicken.

When chickens are forced to live in such close proximity to one another with no possibility of escape, they become severely stressed. Lynching in the livestock world is most commonly seen in poultry farms, where if one chicken gets sick or develops an external wound, her pen mates will quickly gang up on her and peck her to death. To prevent birds from inflicting mortal wounds on each other, farm managers de-beak them.

It's a process where a small portion of the beak's tip is removed and blunted so that it can no longer cause damage. Bird's beaks are made of keratin, a kind of protein and cutting the beaks does not cause pain. But it's a severely stressful operation all the same. And like all veterinary work, it's a skill.

When I first set eyes upon the de-beaking machine, I thought it looked like a cross between a torture device and an amateur radio. The main part was a metallic hot plate that stood on a waist-level stool. Attached to this were yellow insulated wires running off its back and that were inserted bare into a plug point at the side of the poultry house. It wasn't hard to guess that electric current was meant to heat up the plate so that it could burn the beak off. I was a nervous wreck even before we started. A stool was placed in front of this machine for the operator to sit on.

To de-beak a chicken, you first have to catch it. It wasn't long before a processing line developed naturally. The de-beaking operation involved one bird and one student at a time, so we took turns to sit at the machine while the rest of the group formed a rotating processing line starting inside the pen and leading up to the operator. Those inside the pen were the chicken chasers and catchers – we all got pretty good at catching chickens as they ran past. The squawking bird would be passed from hand-to-hand to the operator.

When it was my turn to de-beak a chicken, I was telling myself two things, "a) Don't burn the chicken, and b) Don't burn your hand." You have to use one hand to restrain the bird by holding the wings behind the chicken's back, as if you were going to handcuff it – this makes it stop struggling. While maintaining that gentle but firm grip on the wings, you use your other hand to cup and hold the beak in a firm closed hold. And then, you push the beak with a steady, steady hand on the hot plate.

The junior lecturer who was in charge gave us some basic tips before we started. "If you push too far, you will burn away the tongue along with the beak," he said. "If you see the chicken becoming pop-eyed the day after de-beaking, you know you've cut too much. You also have to take care to hold the beak at the correct angle; else the upper and lower beaks may be cut unevenly."

Well, forget the bird, I certainly felt like my eyes were popping out of my head as I restrained the chicken and took my seat.

With a silent prayer, I applied my chicken's beak on the hot plate, taking care not to allow any part of my hand to touch it. As the yellow beak touched the hot plate and burned, the tip curled and turned black and I hurriedly withdrew my bird. The junior lecturer was standing by watching, and he instructed me to try again.

Again, I pushed my bird's beak on the plate and again it fizzed and burned. I drew back. "Tava tikak," said the lecturer in Sinhala. "Again, a little bit more."

One more time, I applied the chicken's beak on the plate and kept it in position for a second or two, then withdrew.

"Tava," repeated the instructor.

Again, I pushed and withdrew. By this time, sweat was running into my eyes and causing them to burn.

"Tava," came the voice of the instructor.

One final time I applied the bird's beak to the hot plate and withdrew. This time, the instructor was satisfied that the beak was trimmed to the desired level. With relief, I stood up and put my chicken back in the pen. As I re-joined the chicken-catching-and-forwarding line, I hoped I'd never have to de-beak another bird in my life.

It was a hot day and the whole process took a good two hours. Every now and then there would be a sudden commotion, and amidst a thrashing of wings and legs and flying feathers, a chicken would escape the operator's grip and run. One more time we would chase and catch the escaped convict and start the whole process again.

Looking back, I can't remember if there was a specific point in time when I knew. But it was one of life's easy decisions. Poultry doctoring was definitely out.

—

Being a dairy veterinarian was probably the second option that I threw out of the window. Similar to the poultry industry, the dairy industry was seen as a sunrise industry for Sri Lanka, holding a lot of potential for revenue and job creation for the island. It was being promoted by a number of government programmes, and there was even a vision document floating around that had set out a plan for the island to become self-sufficient in milk production. It was, accordingly, given top priority by our veterinary course. Great emphasis was placed on the dairy cow, and we were given comprehensive training in the classroom and in the field. Starting from the very first year, we students were taken on countless trips to dairy farms and spent innumerable hours examining and diagnosing medical cases and doing pregnancy evaluations in barns that ranged in size from tiny three cow operations to gigantic agribusinesses with enormous, specially-designed barns and thousands of cows.

I couldn't help thinking that it wasn't much of a life that these cows had. Beyond all my distress at the doomed lives that they led, I soon discovered that being a dairy vet was bloody hard work. Tramping in gum boots for hours every day through dung-filled barns, cleaning hooves, doing pregnancy exams, and examining cows was a physically demanding job. One got used to it, I suppose, and it paid well, just like the poultry industry. Veterinarians doing dairy and poultry work in Sri Lanka were among the highest paid, alongside perks like a jeep with petrol allowance, free housing, and free food.

But when it came to quality of life, there wasn't much to write home about.

No, no. I wasn't the right person to be a dairy vet. There was no question that it had to go.

—

Pig medicine was a whole different challenge. Like any other enterprise where animals are being raised for meat, these pigs would ultimately go under the knife. But there was no need to even go there. I was defeated by the very nature of pigs. In fact, I'm really not sure there is any veterinarian who actually wants to be a pig vet, who just enjoys working with boars and sows and piglets every day.

We went on house calls to a handful of backyard piggeries that were the epitome of random disorder. Usually no more than ramshackle extensions of the farmer's house itself, these pens had tarpaulin or asbestos sheets for partitions. There was no drainage to speak of and all the pigs were thrown together in a haphazard fashion. Wearing just rubber flip-flops, the farmer, his wife, and any available workers moved between the accumulated muck of the pig pens, the cow barns, the goat shed and the poultry houses. Most often, there would be a water pump, sometimes a tap, but they weren't used much. There were probably whole rivers of bacteria and viruses rushing from one animal to another, and to the humans as well. Compared to those backyard operations, modern pig farms are very organised affairs with specialised management practices applied to boars, gilts, sows and piglets. Production lines and management practices are completely different for breeding animals versus those being raised for the butcher.

Visits to pig farms were always action-packed adventures. The moment we entered the farm and dismounted from our college van, we could see them all group together and watch us with raised heads. As soon as we entered the pig house, it was as if the switch of a toy train set had been turned from 'off' to 'on'. They would all start milling about their pen, led by the largest one, with piglets running between their legs, in danger of being crushed from moment-to-moment. About now is when the grunting orchestra would start as well.

Handling pigs is an art in itself. Once we opened the gate and entered any pen, the noise would immediately go up several decibels and the ring-a-ring-a-roses running would become just a tad more urgent. It was always best to enter the pen with a partner, if not as a small group, because there was the constant danger of being attacked, or falling over if a pig bumped against your legs as it ran. The larger sows and boars were the height of a calf and weighed close to 100 kilos, so it paid to have some member of the group watch out for them. We always entered with gum boots – the standard method to ward off any threatening pig was to apply the sole of the boot against its snout.

The only moment of laughter in all my pig doctoring happened on one visit to the teaching farm. Busy catching pigs inside the pen, we heard a sudden yell. I turned just in time to see a member of my group get knocked off his feet by a large sow as she ran. By some chance she ran between his legs as he overbalanced, and our alarm turned to guffaws as she ran past with him riding rodeo-style on her back.

Pigs, and piglets in particular, have loud voices. Seeing how tiny they are in their first few weeks of life, you could never imagine how loud they can be. The only way to restrain a pig (before it reaches adulthood) is to grab its hind feet as it runs past and elevate it, like you would when holding the handles of a wheelbarrow. The thing is, the moment you catch a pig, it starts squealing. And 'squeal' is a misnomer, because it's really a high-pitched scream. To be assaulted by that high-pitched scream at close quarters, when you are trying desperately to control the kicking, writhing pig so that someone can give it a shot, or take its temperature, is a nerve-fraying, cortisol-raising experience that has to be felt to be understood. And it's as if they don't need to pause for breath, because they can keep it up for long minutes on end. Industrial-quality ear muffs – the type worn by factory workers who operate loud machinery – that's what should be mandatory protective gear for all vets working with pigs.

As veterinary students, most of the pig work that we did was routine management, especially for piglets, each time there was a farrowing. This meant a general check-up, teeth clipping, tail docking, an iron injection and castration.

It was best to carry out these procedures in the first three weeks of life, when they were still little. Piglets' teeth are razor sharp and they can cause injury to the sow while suckling as well as to each other. They are therefore clipped as a preventive measure. If the males' incisors are not clipped at the piglet stage, they will soon grow into curved tusks, and the bigger they are – both the boar and his tusks – the more difficult the task of removing them. Similarly, piglets tend to bite each other's tails, causing injury and danger of infection, so stockmen prefer to have them docked. This is done under local anaesthesia with injections of lidocaine. The whole procedure takes no more than minutes in piglets.

Iron shots are another part of the routine care protocol for new-born piglets as the sow does not produce sufficient iron in her milk and is unable to satisfy the piglets' needs. Without iron supplements, the piglets are prone to anaemia. In the old days, stockmen attempted to solve this problem by feeding the piglets iron-rich soil. They would collect the soil and dump it into the pens, and then hope that all piglets got a good share. Nowadays, he calls in the vet to give an iron dextran shot.

Unless the piglet is one of the chosen ones who the stockman plans to use as a breeding boar, it will undergo a castration around the three-week mark. This is done for several reasons in commercial piggeries. For one, stockmen believe that castrated boars are more docile and easier to manage. Second, it prevents unwanted breeding. And finally, the boar's accessory sex glands produce a pungent odour that taints the meat and brings down its value. Once he is castrated, all these problems are avoided.

For all its drastic and rather final outcome, the castration procedure is pretty straightforward. In piglets, it takes only about ten minutes even when done by a novice. It requires two people. One person acts as the surgical assistant and holds the piglet upside down by its hind legs. At the farms we visited, this meant that the poor piglet would be hanging down on one side of the pen, with his hind quarters balanced on the parapet. The surgeon begins by giving injections of local anaesthetic at a few spots into the scrotal tissue and waits a minute or two for it to take effect. After that, the scrotal skin is incised and the testicle is extracted. As students we were taught to apply ligatures on the testicular vessels – then, all that remained was to cut away the ligaments and lift the testicle out. We were taught to apply sutures on the scrotal skin as the last step of the operation, but experienced vets can probably carry out the whole procedure with minimal incisions that do not require suturing.

Beyond discomfort and their general dislike of being handled, the piglets seemed none the worse for wear due to the procedure and would scamper away as soon as they were let down.

One time when we visited the teaching farm, the clinician informed us that there was a pig to be castrated. He was a teenager, probably four months old, and weighed between 40 and 50 kilos. He had somehow been missed when all his brothers and cousins were being castrated and had only been discovered when his scrotum had attained adult size and became too prominent to miss.

The procedure was the same as that for piglets. But due to his size, aggression, and weight, it took an extreme effort, right from capturing, to lifting, to incising all the tissue and applying sutures. We had to take turns to hold him as he was too heavy for one person to hold him throughout the operation, which took a good twenty minutes.

It didn't take long at all for me to realise that while I'd always be happy to treat individual pigs, being a pig veterinarian and treating them day-in and day-out was not an option. In fact, I don't think the specialty even exists... there are dairy vets and equine vets and small animal vets. Even vets who specialise in exotics – animals like guinea pigs and iguanas. But I don't think there is a pig vet specialty. With good reason, too.

And so, as I moved through veterinary college, my choices for a career path became narrower, but clearer. There was always small animal work, although I realised that I was getting greedy and wanted something more than the regular work with dogs and cats. Then there was the option of going back to my first love and being a vet to zoo animals, although I was worried that jobs in that specialty would be hard to come by. I hadn't had enough exposure to horses, but what little I had at the teaching farm had been enough to confirm what I had long suspected – that I was congenitally in love with horses. I needed some rough and tumble experiences being a horse doctor to gauge if the equine veterinary lifestyle would suit me. And besides, I had my own doubts about the quality of life of the horses in stud farms.

But, no matter. The canvas was still wide open and filled with interesting possibilities.

Chapter Nine

Highs and Lows

I don't know if there is any other profession like veterinary medicine that lifts you to the skies one moment and then unceremoniously drops you to the earth the next, with such cold regularity.

It happened time and time again. I'd be walking on air because of a correct diagnosis I had made, or because of having discharged a patient from hospital. Just a few hours later, I'd be hiding in the changing room, feeling crushed and worthless due to an error in judgement so basic that I'd question my competence.

It is true that identifying a cat's gender can be surprisingly hard. Scores of pet owners come to the veterinarian believing that their cat is about to litter, only to find out that their queen is actually a tom cat. But what do you say about a veterinarian, even one in training, who makes mistakes in telling a tom cat from a female?

My neighbour's family had adopted a kitten whom they christened Chooty. 'Chooty' in Sinhala means 'the little one', and every third pet in Sri Lanka seemed to be named Chooty. This included some like a 60 kilo mastiff that was anything but 'chooty'. In the first six months of his life, Chooty was a privileged visitor to my apartment. Especially during weekends when I'd be at home, it was a delight to have him jump casually into my apartment through my living room window, mewing his greeting. Like all kittens, he was a natural clown and was wonderful company, curling around my legs as I cooked, lying next to my face on my bed— which he quickly took over as his own— or chasing imaginary beings in wild, crazy runs around my apartment. I had had ample opportunity to examine Chooty during those early months and I knew that he was a male.

Sadly, once he became an adult, his personality changed and he became more interested in hunting in the garden and in regular brawls with the neighbourhood cats. On a couple of occasions when he came visiting, I was horrified to see him spray-marking the curtains. That just wouldn't do and I banned him from entering my apartment after that.

One morning, when I had just finished my breakfast at the hospital's canteen, my friend walked up to inform me that 'some people downstairs' were asking for me. I walked down to the reception area to find my neighbour and his wife sitting there. As always, they beamed when I walked up.

"Hello Dilan, Malini," I greeted them. "What's the matter?"

"We have brought Chooty," answered Malini. "We want to do an ultrasound and check if she is pregnant."

"But Chooty is a male!" I said.

"No, no. She's female. I'm sssuuure of it," insisted Malini.

She was now looking at me with an expression that melded sympathy with contempt in equal measure. And now it all came back to me. I had always heard them referring to their pet cat as "she". I had wondered why but then dismissed it without too much thought.

There was one sure way to put the matter to rest.

"Have you brought Chooty with you?" I asked.

"Yes," replied Dilan. "She's in the car."

"Okay, why don't we go take a look at her?" I said. "Then we can be sure."

Accordingly, we all walked out to the car park. Dilan opened the back door and took Chooty out of his basket. Cats should never, ever be examined in the open because even the most domesticated cat can get spooked by a random noise or by the sight of a dog, and suddenly run away. It was thus with some trepidation that I held Chooty in my hands while staying inside the car. Turning him over, I took a good look at his perineal region, and sure enough, I could clearly see the two scrota in place, even though they were not very prominent and were covered in fur.

"Well, as far as I know, Chooty's a male," I declared. "But since you have come, why don't you get him examined by the clinician today? Then we can all be doubly sure. Just make sure that they check his gender before preparing him for an ultrasound, it will save a lot of time."

They agreed and I was late for my 8 AM morning lecture. So taking my leave, I rushed up to class. I only half-listened to the lecture, because I was in a state of mild tension. By some remote chance, if Chooty indeed turned out to be female, I would look pretty silly. And what's more, my reputation with my neighbour's family would be tarnished for life. It would be a loss of face on a Himalayan scale.

At 8.45 AM, just as my lecture ended, my phone beeped. It was a message from Dilan. "You are absolutely correct," said the text. "Chooty is a male. Thank you for all your assistance."

"No problem," I messaged back in elation. "Glad I was able to help."

If my chest swelled with self-importance from that incident, it was comprehensively deflated the very next day. A client came to the OPD with her cat, who, she complained, had been dull since the previous day and had refused all her favourite foods.

I took the patient into the cat examination room and slid the door shut. After asking the client the usual questions about any possible change in diet, whether the cat was an indoor or an outdoor cat, and if she had seen any diarrhoea or vomiting, I began my examination of the cat.

This is the time when I would check if the patient was a male or a female cat, and we were trained to check, even if the owner seemed informed and confident of their cat's gender. Picking up the cat, I looked at the belly and perineal region closely. Nope, there was no scrotum there, so the lady was right, her cat was indeed a female.

There was no temperature and the patient seemed alert and responsive. It seemed to be a routine case of food allergy. Accordingly, I walked out and went in search of Dr. Roshan, the clinician who was on duty that day. Explaining the case to him, I suggested that we just prescribe sucralfate, advise the owner to stop feeding her pet for 24 hours, and then re-evaluate.

"Hmm," replied Dr. Roshan, as he walked-ran in his customary way to the cat room, with me hurrying behind him.

As we entered the cat room, he asked me if I had checked if it was a male or a female. "Yes," I answered, "it's a female."

Dr. Roshan began his examination looking at the mucosae in the mouth and palpating the abdomen. He asked a series of questions in Sinhala to the client while he was doing so. As he palpated between the hind quarters of the cat, he suddenly stopped and turned to me.

"You think this is a female?" he asked.

"Yes," I replied, the alarm bells in my head starting a slow chime.

"Did you palpate?"

"Yes," I answered in a small voice. Now the bells were clanging away in right earnest.

"Come here, give me your hand," said Dr. Roshan. He grasped the forefinger and thumb of my right hand. "Feel here," he said, and he made a palpating motion with my fingers at a spot in between the cat's hind legs.

Sure enough, there was a tiny scrotal sac hidden in all the skin folds and fur, and inside were two small testicles. The cat was male.

"Always palpate!" came the next dictum from Dr. Roshan. "Ok, go ahead, write the prescription and bring it to me," he said as another student came in and called him to the next patient. But he had one last word for me.

"Female? Hmph!!" he snorted as he left the cat room.

It was a good time to slink away to the cafeteria and fortify myself with a cup of tea.

—

By the middle of our seventh semester, we were properly into the grind of daily rounds and patients at the teaching hospital. We were learning on the job, to interact with pet owners and get a proper history of the case from them. The whole process was a source of tension for me since I didn't speak Sinhala. But I had by then worked out a method of communicating with clients using a mixture of broken Sinhala and gestures, aided by the few words in English that they spoke. There was a small percentage of clients who did not understand a single word I was saying and vice versa. On such occasions, I'd enlist the help of a classmate. In the same way, when I had to give instructions to clients about peri-operative protocols and make sure they didn't feed their pet before the next day's surgery, or if specific medication or care instructions had to be communicated, I'd always call a friend to explain the matter, to avoid miscommunication.

One gets to experience the entire galaxy of human personality types inside a veterinary hospital. Some clients were gruff, some were in awe, but most of them were polite and appreciative of the work we were doing. Some left the hospital shouting that we had killed their pet, others had cakes delivered to us. Some sat and bawled when their pet died inside the hospital; others lashed out and questioned the competence of the doctors, and several others thanked us for all we'd done for their pets, through streaming tears. When a pet was discharged, some clients would ask for the bill, pay, and leave without a word. Others would ask us our names and thank us profusely before leaving us bathed in their gratitude.

Somewhere along the way, I came up with an unproven theory in which I related the behaviour of the owners to the prognosis of their pet. I had come to believe that if the client was rude or difficult to manage, the case would most likely have a good prognosis and end with the patient getting better. On the other hand, when the clients were lovely people – the type who treated even us students as if we were experienced doctors – it seemed almost inevitable that the outcome would be poor. It was just random raving by my work-stressed brain of course, but it seemed to happen time and time again.

When I look back on one such case, the total length of my interaction with Genie and her family was no more than two days. But it was two days of sadness and defeat from the beginning to the quick end.

I first met Genie on a Sunday when I was assigned the ICU case. Genie was a fawn Labrador, just emerging from puppyhood. She had respiratory distress of unknown cause, and when I met her, she sat underneath an examination table, fighting for every breath and looking completely miserable. Due to her dyspnoea, she could not lie down comfortably on her chest, but had to sit up. She'd change position every few minutes in an attempt to breathe easier.

I looked at her file. They had started her on a bronchodilator and put her on antibiotics. A blood test had been done and X-Rays taken. All diagnostics had come out inconclusive. She was put under continuous monitoring, and the oxygen tank and mask were kept at hand for any episodes of increased dyspnoea, or if

Genie showed signs of severe distress.

The bottom line was that we didn't know what the hell was wrong with her.

Then Genie's family came to see her. There was dad, mum and three young girls whose ages ranged from eight to eleven or twelve. Full of old-world courtesy, the parents greeted me with warm smiles and respect in spite of their distress at the condition of their pet.

"How is she, Doctor?" asked dad.

If it had been a few weeks earlier, I would probably have tried to be vacuously optimistic and given dad and mum false hope. I had handled a case just a few days ago, of a Pomeranian pup that had entered the OPD struggling to breathe and so anaemic, that his buccal mucosae were an even white instead of pink. On that occasion I had given the poor owner hope based on little more than unfounded optimism and my towering lack of experience.

"He's young," I had assured the owner. "There is a chance that he will respond to treatment. We'll keep him under continuous monitoring." I thought I was making the owner feel better with my positive talk as we wheeled the pup into the ICU. Five minutes later, the puppy was dead. We didn't even have a chance to hook him up to the oxygen.

So when Genie came in, I knew that respiratory distress was a dangerous sign. I wasn't about to make the same mistake again.

"I'm afraid it's not looking good," I answered. "Whenever a dog has difficulty in breathing to this extent, it worries me. I'm sorry, but she is very sick."

Their faces fell and mum looked like she was fighting back tears.

"What has caused this, Doctor?"

And there it was. What indeed? "We have done a number of tests but they are not showing anything specific. The x-ray also does not show anything in her lungs that would explain her breathing trouble," I replied.

"Right, Doctor," said mum and dad together.

"For now, we've given her an antibiotic as well as something to ease her breathing and to keep her as comfortable as possible."

"Okay, Doctor," the couple said in one voice.

"We'll keep her under constant watch."

"Right, Doctor," they chimed.

They seemed satisfied with my answers and there really was nothing more that I could tell them.

They stayed on for some more time with their beloved pet and I got busy with other patients in the ICU. After about an hour or so, mum came to let me know that they were leaving and would be back on the morrow to see Genie.

"You'll keep an eye on her, will you, Doctor?" She looked up at me with a touching mixture of worry, faith, and supplication. I had seen such an expression before only on my mother's face when she would stand in front of the deity at the temple, oblivious for a few moments to everyone around her.

"We'll do our best," I answered.

"It seems she has to be here overnight, Doctor?" she asked.

"Yes, it's best that way, so we can keep a watch on her and continue the medications."

"Who'll be here during the night, Doctor?"

"I'm on night duty tonight, so I'll be here," I replied.

"Oh, fine," she answered, visibly relaxing and giving a small, tired smile. "You'll call us if there is anything, Doctor?"

I promised her that I would. With that, she took leave.

The girls came in next, one by one, to say goodbye to Genie. The eldest came in first, sat down next to Genie and spoke to her in low gentle tones before throwing her arms around the dog and hugging her. The second girl came in next and repeated the performance. The little one came in last and said goodbye with hugs and kisses.

I settled down to fill in some patient files. But the door swung open and the eldest girl came in again. The whole sequence was repeated a second time, as one by one, the girls came in and said their goodbyes for the night to their beloved Genie.

"This," I told myself, "does not look good."

A tragedy was unfolding before my eyes and I felt like there was absolutely nothing I could do about it.

Genie's symptoms continued all night – she would sit down and get up, sit down and get up every few minutes in a futile attempt to breathe easier; and right through, her laboured breathing could be heard even outside the ICU. It was heart-breaking and I felt like I was growing smaller by the minute. Here we were in a referral hospital, no less, and we could do nothing to help this poor dog. Aminophylline usually did its bronchodilatory work well. I couldn't understand why it had had no effect whatsoever on poor Genie. I called the on-call clinician to take a look at her but we could think of nothing else to make her feel better.

The end came early in the morning at around 5.30 AM. One last time, she lay down on her side, and this time she didn't get up, she just faded away. I called out her name and reached for my stethoscope, but I already knew that Genie was dead.

With great weariness I stood up and woke up the on-call clinician to inform him of Genie's passing. My feet didn't seem to want to move when I lifted her body and placed her on the trolley near the back entrance, as was customary when a patient died. Corpses could not be left in the ICU for fear of spreading infection to other patients.

By now it was 6 AM and I went back to the ICU, picked up her file and started walking over to the reception to call the owners. I didn't need to. As I walked up the corridor and looked out of the window at the growing light, I saw a jeep pull into the hospital's parking lot. Genie's family was here, and a few moments later, mum walked through the front entrance.

"Good morning, Doctor," she wished me.

I don't think I even had the courtesy to return her greeting. Discomfort sometimes makes us brusque. "I'm afraid the news is not good," I told her.

"Okay, Doctor," she said looking up at me and the tears had already started rolling down her cheeks. I suppose my expression had conveyed the news.

"I was just coming to call you," I said. "About half an hour ago, Genie passed away."

"I'll just call my family," she mumbled, turning to go out and call her husband who seemed to be turning the jeep to go drop his daughters in school.

The jeep stopped and the eldest girl jumped out first, sensing something was amiss. The whole family seemed to have this ability to read expressions well, because she saw her mom's face, and her own face crumpled. Running to her mom, she hugged her. Dad pulled the car back into the parking spot and they all trooped in.

I know I walked up to dad, shook his hand, and spoke something for a few minutes about Genie's last night, but I wouldn't be able to tell you what I said. My only memory is of his face and his struggle to keep the tears from flowing out uncontrollably.

I led them to where Genie's body lay and the three girls ran up to the body. I thought they would never stop bawling. The parents stood behind them, crying silently.

There were certain formalities to be done even in a moment like this. I approached dad and mum again.

"What would you like us to do?" I asked. "If you would like to take her body with you, that's fine, or we can take care of the body for you."

"What do you do with the... the bodies?" asked mum.

"Normally, they are cremated," I said. It seemed like a more appropriate word than 'incinerated'. Corpses were put in the incinerator.

Mum seemed to be okay with that, and turned to dad to see what he thought. Dad shook his head at her. "No, we'll take her," he said.

"All right, I'll just pack up her body for you," I said and they agreed.

I had done it a few times before and it never got easier. I cut out the tapes on her foreleg and removed the intravenous line that had been set there. I then cleaned up the body as best as I could and fetched a couple of black body bags and tape. Dad helped me and together we put Genie's remains into the bags, which I taped tightly shut.

Dad said he would pull up the car to the back entrance, and once he was there, I carried Genie's body to the car. I placed it as gently as I could in the back seat which they had cleared up.

It was time for goodbye. Dad came up and shook my hand, thanking me for all I had done. "I'm so sorry for your loss," I told him and mum, who was standing next to him. They were gracious as usual in their grief and still seemed to hold veterinarians in high regard. In any case, their innate good nature and breeding wouldn't allow me to think otherwise.

The denouement was as unexpected as it was brutal. Mum called the girls over.

"Say thank you to the Doctor," she said.

"Thank you, Doctor," chorused the girls through their tears and misery. This was more than I could handle and I just about managed to maintain my composure. I also felt I had to say something to console the girls, no matter how shallow it sounded.

"We're so sorry we couldn't save Genie," I told them. They just continued sobbing. Finally, dad and mum said goodbye and they left with the remains of their dog.

It was about 7.15 AM now and I dragged myself to the OPD. Thankfully, I had a few minutes to gather myself before my classmates arrived for morning attendance.

The grief of a child is a very terrible thing. It seemed to me that a child who is too young to have known death, loves her pet with such ferocity that when it dies, the shock and pain are almost too intense to bear. But children are also supposed to be extremely resilient, able to absorb such grief and move on with their lives.

I hoped that was true.

—

Rotations in the hospital's OPD were always tiring and stressful for us students. The teaching hospital received a daily average of sixty cases at the OPD, and I'd often see some patients waiting for the OPD to open when I walked in at 7 AM in the morning to start my shift. By nine o'clock, the reception and waiting area would resemble a fish market with a crush of owners waiting with their pets while the doctors rushed about from one case to another. We had to spend three weeks at the OPD each semester of our final year, and it was a massive relief when I finally finished my second rotation at the OPD. I still had two more rotations to complete at the surgery and at the farm before the end of the semester, but I was ready to celebrate.

However, that wasn't the last of my OPD experiences at the teaching hospital, not yet...there was one final hurdle to be crossed. In our final exams at the end of semester eight, one of the papers was small animal medicine. Out of all the subjects – large and small animal surgery, reproduction and obstetrics, large animal medicine – we knew that small animal medicine was the most difficult to pass. It had a practical section as well.

The practical exam was devastating in its simplicity and horror. The exam was to be a real case at the OPD.

Your rotation group would have to be present at the OPD on the assigned day. The team of examiners would also be present, and they would randomly assign visiting pet owners and cases to students. The nature of the cases ranged from the relatively simple ones that would have straightforward diagnoses and be completed within hours, to things like vestibular syndrome that required hospitalisation and that could go on for days. If you got a complicated case, tough luck; you just had to stay on it until the patient either died or was discharged. If your patient died, you had to close the case by doing a post-mortem and reporting the results. It was diabolically unfair on the students who were stuck for days, sometimes weeks, with a case while others walked jauntily off from the hospital two hours after taking their case. But that was how it was. All you could do was to bite the bullet and pray that you got a 'good case'.

I had an added worry: what if I got a case where the owners didn't speak any English? My Sinhala was still non-existent for all practical purposes. If I couldn't get a proper history from the owners, how would I even fill in the evaluation form, never mind make a diagnosis? Was I about to lose marks because of my inability to communicate? I couldn't exactly call one of my classmates for help here as I used to do at regular OPD.

All these thoughts swirled about in my head when I heard one of the examiners call my name. Well, this is it, I told myself. Whatever it is, there's one sure way to find out.

I walked up to the reception desk where one of the examiners was standing.

"Krishnaswamy. Take this case," he said, indicating a couple who were standing by with their brown Doberman.

"Please come into the OPD, sir," I said to them, hoping that my nervousness didn't show.

The man came close to me and said with a worried look, "Our dog Ansie's not been eating well, Doctor."

And immediately, I began to feel better. He spoke English. Half the battle was already won.

"Oh, is that so?" I replied.

"Yes, Doctor." Then he came even closer and whispered: "And she's not had her periods Doctor!"

"Ohh?" I said, backing away a little. "Well, do come in sir, and let's take a look at her," I told him, ushering him and his wife to an available table.

They hoisted Ansie onto the examination table and, picking up my evaluation form, I began taking a history of the case from them while taking a good look at my very woebegone patient. Ansie was a sweet-natured, two-year-old brown Doberman, but at the moment she was in a state of extreme depression. She lay on the table with a miserable expression on her beautiful face.

Mr. Fernando did all the talking, his wife didn't speak English. They had had Ansie since she was a pup and she was normally a cheerful and hyperactive dog, he told me. She had littered two months ago. Ten pups, Mr. Fernando told me proudly. She had been fine after the whelping and returned to her normal activity levels. Then suddenly, about ten days ago, Ansie had started going off her food. Now she was barely eating anything, and no amount of coaxing with her favourite foods would make her eat. Her water intake was okay. She had stopped playing and just lay about all day, as she was doing on the examination table. And yes, she had missed her heat. They had driven 150 kilometres to bring her to our hospital and clearly loved their dog like their own child.

I had seen cases like Ansie at the OPD before – the same extreme depression, looking with complete apathy at the world, a history of anorexia, the pale mucosae and a history of ticks. I hadn't even started my physical examination, but I knew what was wrong with Ansie.

The exercise, which had started out in high tension, now turned to calm, and felt like an ocean of serene little waves.

I began my physical examination and, like a dream, all the symptoms showed up one by one. I recorded them on my form. Pale anaemic mucosae, not jaundiced yet. Swollen lymph glands. An enlarged spleen. The temperature at 102.9 Fahrenheit was only borderline high, but in real life, patients didn't always show each and every classic symptom mentioned in the textbooks.

The history, anaemia, and splenomegaly were already enough for me to make a diagnosis. It was an open-and-shut case. Poor Ansie had babesiosis, known colloquially as tick fever.

After taking Mr. Fernando's permission, I clipped a small amount of hair from the tip of her ear and made a pin prick there to collect a sample of blood on a slide. I took the slide to the laboratory and looked at it under the microscope.

There they were. The characteristic signet-ring pattern of the Babesia gibsoni parasite was plainly visible inside the red blood cells. They had invaded Ansie's red blood cells after being transmitted by blood-sucking ticks, and were now destroying them. Hence the anaemia and extreme fatigue.

I triumphantly labelled my slide and carried it back to the OPD. My case was almost finished. All I had to do was report my findings to the examiner and advise Mr. Fernando on what to do.

But before that, there was one item left to close the case. I had taken a sample of Ansie's blood and submitted it to the hospital's lab for a full blood count and analysis. Once the sample was submitted, the lab technician put it first into a centrifuge, and next into the automated analyser. It took about twenty minutes for the results to be printed out.

I walked over to the laboratory and gave the technician my patient's name. She looked at her pile of just-printed reports, and selecting Ansie's, she handed it to me.

"Very severe anaemia," she commented, somewhat helpfully.

I quickly glanced over the reported parameters as I walked back to the OPD and my patient.

Ansie's numbers were indeed very low; the technician was right. Her PCV was down to a dangerous 10%. Clinicians use these figures to classify patients from mildly anaemic at 20-25%, to severely anaemic when the PCV is between 10 and 20%. Anything below was classified as critical. With her PCV at 10%, Ansie wasn't just severely anaemic, she was borderline critically anaemic.

From a clinical standpoint, this dangerous level of anaemia normally meant that the patient was given a transfusion of blood to tide over the critically low blood levels in her body. My brow furrowed with worry again. This meant conducting a blood typing operation on Ansie, finding a donor with the same blood group, collecting the donor's blood, and finally carrying out the transfusion.

It was time to have a discussion with Ansie's parents, Mr. and Mrs. Fernando. Blood report and blood smears in hand, I walked back to the OPD, where the couple were waiting patiently for me.

I explained to Mr. Fernando that Ansie had tick fever, how it was transmitted by ticks, and how the parasite was destroying her RBCs. I told him that since the circulating red blood cells carry oxygen and nutrition to body tissues, the severe drop in RBCs was what caused Ansie's extreme fatigue and lack of interest in play and food.

I then showed him the blood reports and explained that her blood levels were dangerously low.

"We recommend doing a blood transfusion, Mr. Fernando," I told him. "Are you willing to let us carry out the procedure?"

"Oh, a blood transfusion?" he said and his eyes were wide with fear.

"Yes, please don't worry. It's a fairly routine procedure...we take a sample of blood from a donor, make sure that the blood groups match, then transfer the blood to the patient. It's just like how we do it for humans who need blood," I told him.

He turned to his wife and they had a quick exchange in Sinhala. From the tone and gestures, it looked like they weren't too enthused with the idea of transfusing blood into their beloved pet. Mr. Fernando turned back to speak to me and a practical difficulty emerged.

"How long will it take, Doctor?" he asked.

"Well," I answered, "we first have to find a donor, that's what can sometimes take a day or two. Then the blood matching and transfusion can be done in a few hours. So if we find a donor immediately, the whole process is likely to take until the end of today, about four-to-five hours. The transfusion has to be done at a controlled, slow rate, so that also takes time."

"Ohh, Doctor, the thing is, we have come from very far away and we have to return anyhow by tonight," he said. "Is there any other alternative?"

"The thing is, Ansie is quite critically anaemic," I replied. "So we shouldn't let her go on much longer without correcting her blood parameters."

"Yes, yes, I understand Doctor. We will do anything for Ansie," replied Mr. Fernando. He thought for a bit and explained what I had said to his wife. One more quick exchange later, he asked, "Doctor, can we do further treatment with our local town doctor? Maybe if you write the medicines or procedures, we can ask him to do it?"

"Hmmm... that might be possible," I said.

This was beyond my brief and I thought it was a good time to call the examiner over, explain my findings to her, and ask her whether we could do as Mr. Fernando requested.

"Let me call the clinician on duty, sir," I said. "Then we can decide on what to do."

When my examiner walked over to the table, I showed her my report and explained my findings.

"All signs point towards Babesios," I told her.

"Did you take a blood smear?" she enquired.

"Yes," I answered. "It was positive for Babesia."

"Okay, please submit your slide along with your report," she said. "So what have you planned as treatment?"

"I would like to put the patient on a course of Imidocarb and Doxycycline," I answered.

"All right, write up the prescription and bring it to me for signature," she said.

"There is one issue," I said. "The patient's PCV is critical, but the owners have requested that they carry out further treatment at their hometown, as they have come from very far away. They can't stay for a blood transfusion."

"Oh, is that so?" she replied, following it up with a rapid-fire discussion in Sinhala with Mr. Fernando. When he told her the name of their town, my examiner reacted with a loud exclamation of shock.

"Yes, yes," she began turning to me. "It's not practical to do a blood transfusion for this patient. Let us write them a prescription for Erythropoietin, so that they can buy it locally and have their doctor administer it there. Please include a vial of Erythropoietin in the prescription, to be repeated after 10 days."

I nodded in agreement as she walked off.

"Okay, it's fine sir," I said, turning to Mr. Fernando, as I gathered my evaluation report and blood reports. "I will write you a prescription for Ansie and you can carry out further treatment with your local doctor."

Mr. Fernando and his wife had relaxed again by now and the beam was back on his face.

"Where are you from, Doctor?" he asked.

"India," I replied.

"Ohhh, very fine, so nice," said Mr. Fernando. "Are you in your final year?"

"Yes sir," I answered. "We are now having study leave for our exams... in fact this is my exam case for our practical exam."

And then Mr. Fernando said something that made my day, my week, and probably set me up to pass my final exams.

"You will definitely pass, Doctor," said Mr. Fernando, with complete conviction.

"Thank you so much," I said, and rarely have I meant those words so much.

"God bless you, Doctor," replied Mr. Fernando.

I wrote the prescription and a letter to his local doctor with instructions to administer the Doxy and Erythropoietin for three weeks. Explaining again what needed to be done to Mr. Fernando, I extracted a promise that even if Ansie started getting better, he would ensure that she got all her shots and Doxycycline tablets for the full course. I actually didn't have any doubt about their care with Ansie's treatment.

With many words of thanks and gratitude, the couple left the hospital with their dog. My exam case was finished. All that remained was for me to write my report and submit it to my examiner. I would be grilled on the case during my viva, but that was a battle for another day.

It was 11.00 AM when I walked out of the hospital doors and I felt light and peaceful. I had got lucky. My patient's owner had known English. My patient herself had been sweet-natured and not aggressive. Most importantly, it had been a clear diagnosis and plan of treatment. I couldn't possibly have asked for more. I said a silent prayer of thanks as I walked away from the OPD.

One morning, ten days later, I was sitting in my apartment, well and truly into my preparation for my small animal theriogenology paper. After three-to-four hours of studying about oestrous periods and hormonal treatments, pregnancy diagnosis methods, and the histological clues to look for in heat detection, I was saturated. I stood up from the table to make myself a cup of coffee.

It was, I felt, a good time to check on Ansie. I had a photocopy of my evaluation form that I had taken to prepare for my forthcoming viva voce. It had Mr. Fernando's number. I dialled it and a voice at the other end said, "Hello?"

"Hello, is that Mr. Fernando?"

"Hau, Fernando kata karamu," answered Mr. Fernando. "Yes, this is Fernando speaking."

"Hello, sir, this is Anand from the Peradeniya Veterinary Teaching Hospital."

"Ohhhh, hello Doctor, hello Doctor!" boomed Mr. Fernando. Genuine delight and happiness came gushing over the phone line as if he were standing in front of me.

"I just called to ask about Ansie," I told him. "How is she now?"

"Ohhhh. She's doing wonderfully well, Doctor! Playing and running like normal!"

"Is she eating okay now?"

"Oohhhhhh, she's eating very much Doctor! So much she's eating!!"

"I'm so happy to hear that, sir."

"God bless you, Doctor. God bless you."

"Were you able to find the Erythropoietin at the local pharmacy?"

"Ohh, yes, yes, Doctor, no problem!"

"Please make sure Ansie gets her second dose, sir. It's very important."

"Ohhh, definitely Doctor, we will make sure she gets the injection. We gave our doctor here your letter."

"And you are giving the Doxycycline tablets with her food?"

"Yes Doctor, one a day, just like you told us."

"That is excellent, sir. I am so happy to hear that Ansie is better. She is a lovely dog."

"God bless you, Doctor, God bless you."

I hung up feeling wonderfully like a floating cloud. I was ready to face my final exams.

Chapter Ten

Guru

I was walking up the path from the faculty canteen back to class one morning when I heard a voice hailing me from behind.

"Where are you going?" it hollered. I turned to see the familiar figure of my friend, the department's handyman, janitor, and general odd-jobs man, coming up behind me, pushing his bicycle.

"Good morning, Guru," I greeted him. "I'm on my way to class. And where are you going?"

He held up a stack of bills that he had in one hand. "Going to electricity office, then going to gas office, then going to the administration office."

"Oh, is today bill-paying day?" I asked.

"Yes," he said with his customary wide grin, as if the chore of visiting utility offices and paying bills was the most enjoyable thing in the world. With a wave he was off and I carried on to class.

His name was probably Gurusinghe. Everyone called him Guru. He became my friend during my first weeks at the university, when I passed word around that I wanted to purchase a bicycle. Guru was assigned to take me to the local mechanic's shop (to check out some second-hand bicycles) and also to the supermarket (to see some new ones). Ultimately, I found all of them to be of such poor quality that I never purchased a bicycle. Even though he spoke very little English and I spoke no Sinhala, we hit it off immediately and became friends.

He was a five-foot-five-inch bundle of energy. It seemed as if that wiry chocolate frame contained mostly fibre and a little muscle spread around here and there. I once asked him how old he was and he replied, "Sixty-five!" with the trademark wide grin creasing his face.

"And how long have you been working here?"

"Thirty-five years!!" Again, the grin and the exclamation.

I have a feeling both those numbers were vague estimates. To Guru, such things didn't matter a whole lot. I mean, what were a few years this way or that? It was a rare conversation with Guru that wasn't filled with laughter and smiles.

In any case, he was probably around sixty-years-old, and after that first occasion when I accompanied him to the cycle stores, I learned to avoid walking with him because I had to run to keep up.

I don't think he ever knew my name, because in all the years that I was there, he never once addressed or called me by my name. Like all the staffers in the department, he probably just knew me as 'the Indian'.

During my first visit home after I joined the university, I remembered my friend and wanted to take back a gift for him. I selected a black leather wallet, which I hoped would be useful to him.

A few days after returning, I ran into him outside the Farm Animal Health building. He was with one of his colleagues, so I motioned him aside, indicating that I wanted to talk to him.

When we were alone, I told him that I had a small gift for him and handed him the wallet in its white cardboard box. He took it without a word. His expression became grim and I wondered if I had offended him by giving him the gift. With a nod, he walked off.

In the months that followed, things were as usual between us. He would always call out a greeting as he bicycled past, or we would exchange pleasantries when we ran into each other. He never mentioned the gift and I didn't feel like asking as I still wasn't sure what he thought about it.

One morning, during a free period, I walked down to the canteen for a cup of tea. I had just picked up my cup when I felt a tap on my shoulder and turned to see my friend standing there.

"Guru, kohmade?" I asked, using the Sinhala greeting which means "How are you?"

"Honthai," he replied, "I'm fine."

Then he grinned wider than I had ever seen him grin before.

"That wallet you give me is very good!" he informed me, his happiness warming up the whole canteen.

Smiling helplessly in response, I told Guru that I was very glad that he liked it.

"Next time bring me a shirt," said Guru.

"Okay," I replied and now I was laughing.

In so many ways, Guru was my role model. Whether he was sweeping the yard or running an errand, I never saw his enthusiasm flag. Here he was at the age of sixty-something, having spent his entire working life in the veterinary department of that university. He probably started out as a cleaning boy and would retire as a senior janitor. By all conventional interpretations, compared to me, he had nothing. And yet, to me, he seemed a happy man.

I never had long conversations with him – the language barrier and our different schedules precluded that – but I'm sure he had his share of challenges that life threw at him. I didn't even know if he had a family. But Guru gave you the impression that he had found a way to deal with things one at a time, and keep life very, very simple. There was a delightful air of lightness that he carried about with him that was infectious. He showed me the value of a clear-thinking, or better still, a no-thinking (when not required) approach to life.

Chapter Eleven

Pregnancy Diagnosis

When we were two or three weeks into our seventh semester, our farm animal medicine professor took us for a practical session to the department's Skill Lab. It was a large air-conditioned spacious room on the second level of the department building. As we final year students filed in, I cast an interested eye over the accoutrements.

On one of the counters I noticed what looked like a brown dog's leg that was attached to a stand that had a small plastic bag-like structure filled with red liquid. I walked up and examined it. It was indeed a model of a dog's leg with a prominent cephalic vein curving wonderfully clearly around it. It was the venipuncture training model on which students learned how to put needles into the vein to draw blood samples and to place cannulas. The red liquid from the plastic bag was supposed to be blood, so if you did the procedure properly on the model, your syringe would actually fill up with blood, just like in real life.

Standing to one side was a life-sized model of a Friesian cow with amazing attention to detail. A section of her back could be removed to allow students access to the cow's innards. There was a model of a calf that we could place inside the uterus and understand the various foetal positions in the uterus, and practice deliveries. As we were to discover that year, complications of parturition, or dystocia, was a common occurrence.

While delivering baby farm animals, the veterinarian often works blindly by inserting a gloved hand, or finger in the case of small animals, into the vagina. After giving us a quick lecture on the different malpositions that the calf could take in dystocia, our professor divided us into teams of three and sent us by turn to the back of the cow to try and put the theory into practice. The model stood just a shade under six feet at the withers. He would manoeuvre the calf into place while we were outside the room and replace the back of the cow, so that the calf's position was hidden. Then he would call us back and instruct us to first tell him what the problem was, and then correct it before bringing the calf out.

When my team's turn came, I was the first to insert my hand. I wore the parturition glove and poured on a liberal dose of liquid paraffin. "Wow," I thought to myself. "This is like the real thing."

The normal presentation is when the calf is facing forward in the birth canal with its face between its forelegs and with its hind legs tucked up beneath its abdomen. Then, as the cow strains and pushes, it comes out headfirst. Parturition gets complicated when the head turns to one side, or if either of the legs gets bent or stretched in the wrong direction. Sometimes the calf is upside down inside the birth canal with its stomach and legs on top.

The first thing that I could feel as my hand entered the vaginal canal was the tail of the rubbery model calf. The next thing as per protocol was to feel for the anal reflex, both to confirm that it was indeed the tail you were touching, and not a nostril for example, as well as to check if the calf was alive. Accordingly, I palpated around the anus (yes, the model had one). From there, it was pretty straightforward. Moving my hand a little up and further along, I could feel the back of the calf. Drawing my hand a little back and to the sides, I could feel the legs on either side, stretched lengthwise along the body and towards the head.

So the calf was back-to-front, instead of being front-facing, and its hind legs were stretched forward instead of being tucked up underneath its body.

"Dorsal breech presentation, bilateral flexion of the hip joint," I announced confidently.

"Okay – and how are you going to correct it?" asked the professor.

"First we have to correct the position of the hind legs, then we pull out the calf," answered my teammate.

"Right, go ahead," said the professor.

There are two ways to correct this – using ropes, or by hand. If the cow is small with a narrow birth canal, the recommended way is to fix a loop of rope around the fetlock joints on each leg. This can be done with one hand. Then you insert two hands into the vagina. As your teammate pulls on the rope from behind, you use one hand to pull the knee joint backwards with gentle pressure, while the other bends and tucks the fetlock. It's important for the two team members to work with smooth coordination to bring the leg into correct position. The procedure is repeated for the other leg.

In our case, we found that the model's birth canal allowed enough room to do the procedure without ropes. Inserting both hands, I could manoeuvre the hip and fetlock together in one action to bring the leg into the correct position.

Once we had the calf in the correct position for delivery, it was a matter of pulling it out. Since the hind portion is typically wider than the shoulders and the head, the advantage with a breech presentation is that once the back comes out, the front follows easily and there is little danger of the front getting stuck at the pelvic rim. Taking positions, two of us pulled in turn until the tail and hind quarters emerged. Then we each took hold of a leg while the third member got hold of the tail. With gentle and sequential tugs, we had the model calf out in minutes. Holding it up by its hock joints, we cleared its nostrils, rubbed it down, and gave it a few vigorous slaps on its flanks. It was a successful delivery.

It had been hard work, and yet, this had been a nice big model in an air-conditioned room where there was no danger of either the mother or the calf dying. Later in the term during my ambulatory rotation, I saw the vet slogging through some difficult cases, and I began to understand the incredibly tough conditions under which field vets have to work, often with no help, and with minimal equipment. My respect and admiration for rural field vets grew during that term.

It was in the same Skill Lab that we got our introduction to pregnancy diagnosis. The vet must insert his or her arm into the cow in order to palpate the reproductive tract and check if she's pregnant or not. There was a special pregnancy diagnosis kit to help train novices like us. It was a box-like contraption, about three square feet in size, and about two feet high. With a tube-like rectal tract above and uterus below, ovarian horns and ovaries all made out of rubber, it was a faithful imitation of the actual reproductive tract and extremely useful as a training tool.

Our professor made us stand at the open end of the box while he moved into position at the vulval side and demonstrated how to do a pregnancy check. We could see his hand as he moved it inside the rectum and explained what he was doing.

"You have to stand sideways to the cow... then it will be easy to insert your arm," he said following word with action and standing side-on with his hip against the cow's rear end. "If you are right-handed, use your right hand, if you are left-handed, use your left hand."

His hand appeared inside the box. We watched as he moved his hands along the reproductive tract until he could feel the bifurcation of the uterus. Next, he felt his way along first the left, then the right ovarian horns to their ends and grasped the ovaries near them with his fingers.

"All of you saw the procedure, right? Simple, isn't it? Now all of you practise," said our professor as he withdrew his arm and stepped aside.

We tried it one by one and I thought it was pretty straightforward when I had a go. There was nothing to it – you inserted your hand and there was the cervix, thick and hard. You couldn't miss it as it felt so different from the rest of the tract. After that it was just a step-wise procedure as our professor had showed us. Everyone was smiling at the end of the session... it seemed like those ten marks for pregnancy diagnosis in our farm animal theriogenology final exams were practically in the bag.

Reality struck when we went to the field to try our skills on real cows.

For starters, live cows are very different from a model, no matter how life-like the model may be. What was crystal clear in the lab was just a mushy confusion here. The level of noise – muscles, dung, tissue – all pushing against you – was quite extraordinary. It took many sessions of training before I was able to sort them all out to discern the tract and even start feeling for the ovaries.

Even though the cows we practised on were either at dairy farms or at our university farm and hence quite used to having people feeling about inside them, not all of them were pliant individuals willing to work with you. Some ran while others thrashed about in their stalls as you tried to insert your gloved and soaped hand into them.

By the time we started on pregnancy diagnosis, we were used to working with cows. And that means getting used to having cow dung on you. Actually, cow dung isn't like your normal faecal matter. It's more benign and doesn't stink – I suppose it helps to think that it is after all mostly grass that has come through the cow. But in spite of that, working with dung inside the rectum of a cow still, oddly, took some getting used to. You inserted your hand, and if the colon and rectum were full, your hand went straight into what felt like hot loose clay. Then you had to cup your hand and draw it back, bumping over the rectal folds so that you could take out and discard the dung. You could only start palpating the reproductive tract after clearing the rectum of the dung. During the first couple of sessions, there were many disgusted expressions to be seen as we students repeatedly inserted and drew out bucket-loads of manure.

At least with dung you could feel the cow straining and feel the green clay moving inside the rectum – there was enough time to step clear. But with gas, it was very sudden – there would be regular explosions of methane, and there was little we could do to escape it.

Some of my classmates got the hang of it in no time – they had caught the ovaries and were describing their features in the second class itself. For me, it was a bit of a struggle. I would insert my arm into one cow after another and palpate and search about until my arm hurt as if a truck had gone over it, but I still wasn't sure of any anatomical structure other than the cervix. At the end of those first few trials, I was always frustrated, covered in dung, and depressed – I could feel the cervix fine, but for the life of me, couldn't progress beyond that, no matter how much I tried to tell myself that, logically, all I had to do was keep a hold of that cursed organ and move further along the tubes that led off from it.

But if I was distressed, one of my classmates was having an even harder time of it than I was. About 5 feet tall in her gum boots, Buddhika was one of those girls who was getting bathed in dung and flavoured with methane on a frequent basis. Like me, she also seemed to be not making much progress beyond the cervix – but no matter what, nothing could cloud her sunny personality.

It all finally fell into place for me during a visit to a private dairy farm in Nuwara Eliya for our fourth pregnancy diagnosis practical. I had informed the clinicians that I needed help, and the one who was on the visit with us that day was Dr. Konara. He took me under his wing while my classmates went about their work.

We chose a mid-sized Friesian who stood calmly in her stall as we wore our parturition gloves and lubricated them with liquid paraffin.

"Okay, Anand, you know the procedure... before you start, the most important thing is to be relaxed and take your time without hurry..." said Dr. Konara. "We are here until 4 P.M. today, so you have enough time. I will help you... come, let us start."

As my arm entered the rectum, the cow waggled her rump and gave a desultory kick, before she stood still. I felt the familiar warmth and folded back a few rectal folds. There was no dung and I caught hold of the cervix without any trouble.

"I have the cervix," I said.

"Okay, now keep your hand there – I will insert my hand also," said Dr. Konara and put his gloved arm inside.

Even with one arm inside a cow's rectum, it's a tight fit. With two arms, it was a squeeze. I felt his arm snake alongside mine and soon my arm was getting crushed against the pelvic rim. This was even more painful than when the cow strains, and I groaned in agony.

"Ow, OWW..." I cried out.

"Come on, you have to bear this pain," said Dr. Konara, adding somewhat helpfully, "I'm trying to go past you but your hand is very big."

At that same moment, I heard someone cry out in the background.

"AAI, AAI, AAI," came the shout...I took a deep breath and raised my eyes for a second. I saw Buddhika moving from the left to the right of the stage...she had one hand inside a cow, and with the other, she was holding on desperately to the cow's tail as it ran, dragging her behind it.

Another agonising stab of pain brought me back to my own problems as Dr. Konara finally forced his hand past mine. Pulling it back level with my hand, he grabbed my fingers and guided them as he moved up the tract.

"Okay, so the cervix is no problem. See now I'm taking your hand up the tract – can you feel the bifurcation? The uterine horns?"

And yes, I could feel them – in retrospect, I had probably felt them before, but had been anxious and unsure of what I was palpating.

"Okay now…" continued my coach, speaking with eyes closed in a touching show of concentration, "now see what I'm feeling... can you feel the ovary? Yes. There is no other lymph node or any other structure there – if you feel something solid and ball-like... yes, you know that that is the ovary, and nothing else."

I finally had it – I was holding that elusive ovary in my fingers and it was a nice feeling.

"Wait, let me move. Hold your hand there," said Dr. Konara withdrawing his arm and giving me new variations of the earlier agony. "You have to feel along the tract till you reach the end of the horn... then leave it and JUMP ahead and catch the ovary," said Dr. Konara. He made a small jumping motion right there next to the cow. My hand was inside the cow and I was watching him over her back, but I couldn't help smiling.

"Come on, try to catch it."

I took a breath and started the exploration of the cow's reproductive tract afresh. Just then, I heard Buddhika again. "AAI AAI AAAAIII," came the lusty cries. It really sounded like Buddhika was reaching the end of her endurance and patience. I looked up again, and this time she moved from right stage to left stage. As before, she was hanging on to the cow's tail, but now she was covered from head to foot in dung.

"Did you catch the ovary?" asked Dr. Konara.

And this time, I had caught it all by myself, so I replied with a grin.

"Riiight... then release and catch it, release and catch it, until you feel comfortable. Do the left ovary, then try the right ovary. Now I think you got it, eh?"

He sounded even more satisfied than I was and he moved off to guide the other students.

I kept at it and did as my coach had instructed, letting go of the ovaries and then starting the whole procedure from the start, and I began to feel better about my pregnancy diagnosis skills. There is no definite method to it, one just has to get used to the feel of being inside a cow, and know where to search. After about twenty minutes, I was at the end of my physical strength and I leaned against my cow's side... if I were a dog, my tongue would have been hanging far out and I'd be panting.

Dr. Konara came up to check on my progress.

"What, Anand?" he exclaimed with a smile. "Exhausted? Don't worry – we do dozens of PDs in a day… soon you will get used to it…"

We eventually finished checking that batch of cows and packed our soiled overalls and boots away. There was a general air of fatigue mixed with the satisfaction of a day's work well done.

I caught up with Dr. Konara as we walked up to the canteen to have lunch before starting on the journey back to the campus.

"Thank you, Dr. Konara, for all the time you took to teach me today," I told him.

"Don't say thank you, Anand," said Dr. Konara, grinning in spite of himself and probably understanding the sincerity of my words. "It's my duty."

Many of our most cherished friendships are born in school. I've read that soldiers make lifelong bonds as a result of facing the enemy shoulder-to-shoulder. And some connections are sealed with arms crushed together inside a cow's reproductive tract. It felt like the start of a beautiful friendship with my dairy farm lecturer.

—

Our pregnancy diagnosis practical sessions continued through that semester and the next, but I approached them with more confidence. The practical we had right after the one at the dairy farm was at a buffalo farm close to our campus one hot Saturday morning.

Buffaloes have much smaller tracts compared to cows and the entire reproductive tract lies close to the vulval orifice. Hence, in theory, it is much easier to diagnose pregnancy in buffaloes. With buffaloes, it's also easier to use a technique called ballotment where you push your closed fist against the abdomen and you can feel parts of the foetus bumping against your hand.

The foetus has an artery that supplies it with oxygen-loaded blood. Blood courses through this channel at a rapid pace in the last days of pregnancy, a phenomenon known as 'fremitus'. The instructor encouraged us to feel for it, and as before, there were some students who could identify and feel it right away. I could feel several ovaries this time, but no fremitus.

Anyway, I wasn't worried – I knew that if I kept at it, I would eventually feel the mid umbilical artery and the blood coursing through it, 'like water running through a pipe,' as they all said.

I minded it even less when Buddhika walked up with a big grin of triumph on her face.

"What, Buddhika? Were you able to palpate the ovaries?" I enquired.

"Yes! And I could also feel the fremitus!!" she replied jubilantly.

I congratulated her happily. At last, after all the effort and cow dung baths, we had both found some measure of success.

Chapter Twelve

The Peradeniya Botanical Gardens

Every day, as I rode the bus back home from college, I would go past the botanical gardens that were one of the most prominent landmarks of the town. The entrance archway was right opposite my college's main entrance. I had wanted to go in and have a look ever since I had arrived in Kandy.

I had heard only good things about it and there wasn't a day when I didn't see hordes of foreign tourists and locals visiting. I knew it must be a large area too, because the boundary wall stretched for a good couple of kilometres along the main road. From the bus, I would just get tantalising glimpses of greenery and enormous trees.

However, the schedule of classes was such that weekdays were completely out of the question. And weekends were precious time to catch up on study and do chores like washing clothes and finishing grocery shopping. I suppose if I had really pushed for it, I could have planned a visit sooner. But when the garden is in your neighbourhood, paradoxically, you keep putting off the visit because it's right there and not going anywhere.

My chance finally came after two years. We had just started our fifth semester, and to our pleasant surprise, our subjects that term were relatively light. Those of us who did not have any repeat exams could afford to take it easy.

Makinthan and I decided to watch a Tamil movie one weekend – the latest Kamal Hassan starrer had just been released to rave reviews. During a field trip some months earlier, Makinthan had pointed out a building that looked like a cross between a barn and a factory and assured me that it was a movie theatre that sometimes showed Tamil movies. This movie, we thought, was sure to be running in that theatre.

One Friday, we made our plans and I asked Makinthan to see if any of the motorbike-owning lads would be interested in going – it would solve the transport problem. He agreed and told me to wait for his call the next morning to arrange our meeting point.

"Hi Makinthan, what's the plan?" I asked when he called on Saturday morning.

"Anand, the problem is the movie is not running here in Kandy," replied Makinthan to my disappointment.

"Oh no," I said. "How come?"

"This time they've put it in a theatre in Badulla district," he replied.

"How far away is that?"

"About three hours."

"Well, so much for our movie plans," I thought to myself. "That's real bad luck," I told Makinthan. "Can we do something else today?"

"Like what?" said Makinthan.

"Well, I don't know... we could go to the lake and take a walk," I replied lamely.

"Garden polaamaa?" asked Makinthan, not even bothering to reply to my idea. "How about going to the gardens?"

"Okay, sure," I replied enthusiastically. "Will this rain be a problem?"

It was raining... of course... that day, and I wondered if it was practical to visit a garden in such weather.

"Let's see how it is in the afternoon and then take a call," said my friend.

And so we decided that we would talk again at about 2 PM and see if we could go. It kept raining off and on that day – there would be a light drizzle for fifteen minutes and then the sun would come out with a smile and a wink for the next hour. We decided to chance it, and that's how I finally entered the gardens.

From the first moment, I was glad that we had decided to go. It was every bit as beautiful and charming as I had imagined. Walking pathways ran all around and through the gardens, and Makinthan and I spent a lovely afternoon walking them. Since it was a Saturday afternoon, there were many visitors including several groups of school children being herded by their teachers. But the gardens are spread out over such a large area that often we found ourselves walking along paths with only the trees for company.

And what trees I found there! Different sections of the gardens had cordoned-off areas showcasing varieties of medicinal plants, bamboo, orchids, and so on. There were trees of every conceivable shape and size growing all over the park. I fell in love that afternoon with the trees of the Fabaceae family. They are gigantic trees with trunks so large that you have to walk ten or more steps to complete one circuit around them. Their gnarled roots protrude in zigzag patterns over the grass, and if you look up, their tops and branches completely block out the sky.

One area of the park had the resident population of fruit bats hanging from the tree branches. I was surprised at how large they were since up to that point, I had only seen the small ones that you see flitting about in the evening darkness. They were not shy at all, flying boldly around, and making a healthy cacophony of sound with their calls. You had to walk with care in that part of the park, or you'd be blessed – literally – with a generous dollop of their droppings.

As we neared the entrance again, a group of European tourists passed us. In the group were three or four pretty girls. Dressed in sleeveless tops and shorts, they walked past like a gang of Barbie dolls, all white limbs and curves.

I at least attempted politeness and pretended to look at the plants while admiring them with an oblique glance. Makinthan was wonderstruck and stared openly. His frank admiration meant that his head turned one-eighty degrees as they walked past, so he was soon walking with his head completely turned around facing backwards. At first, I was embarrassed and wanted to tell him not to stare. But I restrained myself.

We'd soon be back in class, in some soul-numbing lecture or other, looking at the same faces day-in and day-out. No, I simply didn't have the heart to say anything to him.

And those girls knew exactly what was going on... they must have been used to it. I could sense them stiffening by minute degrees as they walked by. Behind those dark glasses, I knew they were watching us through slit eyelids.

—

I had just returned to my quarters and finished washing when I heard the front doorbell ringing repeatedly.

I opened the door to see my host family standing there, all alert and present, including Trixy, the newly-adopted kitten clinging on to Preeni akka's shoulder. There was worry in the air, and I could see that something was up.

"Sorry, akka, I was in the restroom," I told her. She could barely restrain herself.

"Trixy fell down from the first floor!" she blurted out.

"Oh really?" I replied as I gathered myself. "Bring him in, let's have a look."

I pried the kitten loose as they all trooped in, and placed him on the coffee table, gently exploring for any obvious signs of damage.

"How did it happen?" I asked Preeni akka.

"I was working in my office when I heard a thud. Running out, I saw Trixy on the floor... when I picked him up, he was bleeding from the nose," she replied. She was the one who had named him Trixy when they adopted him a fortnight ago. Although the others milled about in the background like worried aunts, it was clear that Preeni akka had already become very attached to the little black fellow.

"So nobody actually saw him falling?" I asked.

"No."

"Well, there are no signs of breakage," I said. "He's just a kitten and falls are a part of growing up for them."

I checked his mouth, and didn't see any bleeding or broken teeth. I surmised that the nosebleed must have been due to the kitten bumping his nose while falling. Anyway, the nose was fine and the kitten seemed to be recovering rapidly from any shock he may have had under the attention he was receiving.

"Let's just let him have a walk around and see if there is any damage," I said, putting Trixy on the floor. He immediately set about exploring my living room.

"I don't think there's anything to worry about," I told the worried family. "He may have just had a bit of a scare when he fell, and probably bumped his nose. That's why you saw the nosebleed, but he seems fine now. Just observe his movements tonight, and if you see any nervous signs, like twitching, or any abnormal behaviour, take him immediately to the hospital," I advised, asking, "What is his feeding schedule?"

"Kitten food twice a day," said Preeni akka. "And his milk bowl is usually kept there for him to have whenever he wants."

"Shall we give him a feed of warm milk?" asked Sanath aiyya.

"Yes, I think that's a good idea," I replied.

By now they had relaxed a little bit and the tension had ebbed. I picked up the kitten. "Now, stop scaring everyone, okay Trixy," I mock-admonished him, handing him back to Preeni akka.

The family thanked me and left riding a swell of smiles and relief.

As I drifted off into sleep that night, I could not help thinking that on the whole, it had been a good day.

PART 3

A Newly Minted Vet in South India

Chapter Thirteen

Finding a Roof in Thoothukudi

Soon after graduating from veterinary college and returning to India, I got a job with a non-profit animal rescue organisation in Thoothukudi, a district in the deep south of the state of Tamil Nadu. I had always wanted to explore that part of my home state and it was a good opportunity to gain some experience. I spent a happy year working there.

Finding a decent place to stay in that small town proved to be a major problem. In the first five months I must have seen at least thirty rental places. They generally ranged from lousy to outright terrible. The standard design I observed was to offer literally just one room, with a common bathroom some distance away. Depending on the location, the rent for such places ranged from a ridiculous 5,000 to 8,000 rupees a month.

I was looking for a small apartment with at least one bedroom, a bathroom, and a kitchen. Just the basic amenities would have been fine, I didn't need anything fancy. But in Thoothukudi, all I was finding, weekend after weekend were either high-end houses which were too expensive, or very poor quality dumps where the owners clearly thought that vets and livestock lived in the same way, the one difference being that tenant vets could be bled every month for rent.

One place I saw was especially unforgettable. It was about two kilometres away from the shelter. I was taken to see it by one of the shelter managers in her car.

Once we reached the house, the manager explained to the lady who opened the door that we were there to look at the room. The lady called out to her husband and he came out.

I suppose I should have known this would not end well when I saw him. It was around half-past ten in the morning and he came out unshaven and red-eyed like he had just woken up, in a shirt that he seemed to have hurriedly worn – thank God – and a lungi whose colour I couldn't make out because it was so filthy.

"Come," he said, leading us out and around his house.

The door of the room was locked and while he fumbled for the keys, I took a peek through the window. I could not believe what I was looking at.

The room was packed with broken furniture – I could discern a few broken chairs, and a table, and many wooden planks – strewn all over the floor and stacked up against the wall – caked in what looked like years of dust. Quite obviously the room had been used to store unused items for years. He opened the door and coughing in the dust I moved in a trance through the place. There were two rooms, both in the same state of disuse – he was offering them both for rent. The plaster from the walls lay peeled away in large swathes and the cobwebs added to the overwhelming air of melancholy. There was a tiny room outside and a little away from the annexe, which he said was the bathroom. I didn't even bother looking at it.

The man asked me where I was from and I told him vaguely that I was from up north. To my surprise, he started talking to me in broken Hindi.

"Kidhar se aaye ho?" he asked. – "Where do you come from?"

"Aapne Hindi kahaan seekhi?" – "Where did you learn Hindi?"

"Main Bombay gaya," he answered. – "I went to Bombay."

"Bahut log idhar rehta hain," he declared in a confident tone. – "Many people stay here."

Yes, I'm sure, I thought to myself.

I couldn't leave without asking him how much he wanted for rent. I was trying to convince myself that he really was planning to give out the place for rent, and that he really expected someone to take it.

"How much is the rent?" I asked accordingly.

"8,000," he replied without hesitation.

I turned to the manager who had brought me there.

"Shall we go?" I asked and walked to the car, leaving her to carry out the formalities of leave-taking.

After five months of searching, I found a lovely place to stay. A colleague introduced me to a couple who had a small apartment for rent that was walking distance from the shelter. Being an outhouse to their larger bungalow, it was basic but cosy, and I settled in quickly. Three weeks after I started, I received a note from a friend. Amrita had first been a colleague – she was the communications officer for the non-profit organisation that I consulted with in my previous avataar as an international development consultant. We had kept in touch and now since she was in my neighbourhood, she sent me an email.

"Coming to Thoothukudi on the 8th," it read. "Can you recommend some good places for me to stay? Let's catch up."

My immediate response would have been to invite her over to stay at my place – after all, I had more than enough space. But by then, I had had sufficient exposure to the conservative ways of the deep south. In Thoothukudi, you didn't just invite a member of the opposite sex to stay in your rental apartment.

"Hey Amrita," I replied. "Great to hear that you are coming, and yes, we should definitely meet. It should be ok for you to stay at my place if you are comfortable with it, but let me just check with my landlord. In case he objects, I will suggest a good hotel."

I got my chance to ask very soon. That night itself, my landlord rang the bell to deliver the month's utility bill. With him was his teenage daughter. I thought of her as the Silent One. I first 'met' her when I visited the house to look at their outhouse which they had put up for rent. While I chatted with the owner and his wife, she just sat there and observed me through her Loris eyes. She never spoke a word and never took her eyes off me – it was like being watched by a guard dog. At one point, more out of embarrassment than any real interest, I asked her if she was a student and what she was studying. Her mother assisted me in my efforts with some quick words in Tamil, asking her to be polite and answer the question.

The gaze never wavered. Those big eyes never blinked. She just sat there and watched. At first I thought it was a high level of shyness associated in part with her age, and in part because I was from the big city of Chennai. But that wasn't really it. Even after I had moved in with that lovely family, and in that entire year that I stayed with them, the pattern remained the same. I often saw her going to the market with the housemaid or with her friends, and at those times she was pretty loquacious. During the weekends, when I would be home during the day, I used to see her with her parents as they worked in the garden and every now and then, I'd hear her voice calling to them in a high-pitched screech.

She was a normal teenager, except when she saw me at close quarters. Then, the eyes would grow enormous, and her whole body would go still.

After I had started living there, I often ran into her at the small corner grocery shop, where I went to buy emergency rations of milk, fruit buns, or biscuits. On more than one occasion, she seemed on the verge of greeting me. The head would tilt forward ever so slightly and I was sure I could detect a smile trying its best to emerge. Each time, I would smile and say hello. But when she simply remained staring, I would pick up my bread, nod at her and walk back.

Her parents were a 180-degree contrast. Friendly and garrulous to a fault, they seemed to take an immediate liking to me when I first visited them to look at their outhouse. And a good thing too, because when I met Mr. Sam Lourdusamy and his wife

Philomena, I was desperate to find a homely place that I could return to after the day's work.

And so it was, that that night Mr. Lourdusamy stood there at my door with his daughter. "Hello Anand, I came to give you this month's bill," he said. "Thanks" I replied, then asked, "One thing I wanted to ask you... an old colleague of mine is planning to visit Thoothukudi. Is it okay if she comes and stays here with me?" I made sure I enunciated the gender pronouns.

"But how will you sleep?" asked Mr. Lourdusamy, unhesitatingly, his face creasing into a worried frown.

If the question had been asked in the city of Chennai, it might have been an impolite query.

But with Mr. Lourdusamy, there was no question of taking offense. Of course, he was worried that I was planning some serious debauchery that weekend. And what would the respectable neighbours say if word got out that his Chennai tenant who claimed to be a veterinary doctor had strange women staying with him overnight? But there was no couching of his concerns in a diplomatic "But you have only one bed?" or "Is your friend coming with her husband?" as a worldly-wise, shrewd Chennai or Mumbai landlord might have done. It was a devastatingly simple "But how will you sleep?"

I loved it.

"I will give her my room and I can sleep in the hall," I replied. "Can you give me a spare mattress?"

"Okay," he said after a moment's thought, although he still looked worried. And I could read his mind, as plainly as if a newsreel were rolling across his forehead:

"He *says* he needs an extra mattress, but how do I *know* he's going to sleep separately on it?"

It worked out well in the end. Amrita came and stayed for a night and used my room as planned. Mr. Lourdusamy gave me a thin black foam mattress which I used to sleep on in the living room. In fact, I picked up Amrita after work from the bus stand and by the time we reached home it was past dusk. She was gone by daybreak the next day, so I don't think the gossip hounds even picked up the scent.

There could be no kinder landlords than Mr. Lourdusamy and his wife. They had spent a lot of money and effort in building the outhouse. It was a well-designed furnished apartment with a bedroom, attached bath, a small kitchen with appliances, and a living room, cleverly built to one side of the house, with its own approach gate and entrance.

I liked it immediately and luckily for me, Mr. Lourdusamy and Philomena also seemed to like me. They told me later that no less than 25 other people had visited to see the apartment before me, but they had not been comfortable with any of them. I am really not sure what they saw in me, but I suppose some things are meant to be. Perhaps, after the hardships I had endured over the past five months living in a dump and struggling to find a suitable house, destiny decided to do me a small favour.

Chapter Fourteen

Pet Owners

I suspect that, like me, the vast majority of students, while considering whether their love for animals means they should become veterinarians, completely fail to consider the fact that most animals they treat in future will come connected to a human. They would be well advised to consider this aspect of the veterinary profession very seriously. Unless they enter niche areas like zoo medicine or public health, they will be interacting with pet owners very closely on a daily basis. It can take its toll.

Pet owners are a diverse group... and that's putting it mildly.

During my clinical year at the Teaching Hospital at Kandy, and later while in practice in south India, I met some true characters. The patients were, of course, a total masala mix of sizes, shapes, attitudes and ailments. But here I refer to their human owners. In a very short time, I met pet owners who ranged from the quirky, to the angelic, from those who regarded all veterinarians as charlatans, to some who, I was convinced, had escaped from a mental hospital.

But for sheer force of personality and character that was unabashedly out-there-zany, nothing could beat Mrs. Visalakshi. She seemed to be about sixty to sixty-five years old. With her upright bearing, colourful expensive chiffon saris, large kumkum bindis planted exactly at the centre of her forehead, gentle smile and soft tones, Mrs. Visalakshi was a lady who had presence. Class and breeding oozed out of every pore of her being. And yet, she had a curious trait that simply didn't fit in with that picture, and that popped out during every consultation.

She had adopted a dog from the street many years ago and that puppy had grown into a good-looking, brown-coloured mutt who was about the size of a Labrador. She had named him Bobby. One day when she brought him in, I was on duty along with Dr. Gayathri, a pint-sized, sweet-natured Chennai girl who was my senior. She had graduated from the Madras Veterinary College a couple of years before I had finished my course in Sri Lanka.

As I patted Bobby to calm him down and checked his temperature, Gayathri began asking some questions to get a history.

"Yes, madam, what is the problem with Bobby today?" she asked brightly.

"Ohh, he has not been keeping well these past two or three days. He's not been eating much, and he's not been himself," answered Mrs. Visalakshi.

"Have you given him anything new to eat? Maybe some new treats?" asked Gayathri.

"Oh, no, Doctor, nothing at all...he's been having his usual Pedigree dog food, chicken and rice," came the reply.

"His temperature is normal, so he doesn't have a fever. Does he still eat rubbish from the garden and roadside, Madam?"

"Oh, yes! No matter how much I try, he does that every now and then."

"Hmmm," said Gayathri. "That's probably what is causing the problem now... how is he passing motion?"

"He's been SHITTING LIKE WATER for the past two days... DIARRHOEA," said Mrs. Visalakshi, her voice rising a decibel or two for emphasis. Like a puffer fish under threat, she seemed to have become just a tad bigger in size. In her eyes, I could see a clear challenge.

"Hmmm, anything else, Madam?"

"Yes, he's been FARTING a lot." Again, the tone was high and defiant, and the eyes shone and challenged Gayathri and me.

And there it was. Mrs. Visalakshi had an inexplicable fetish for unladylike words that were completely out of place with her general personality. She'd be talking in her normal tones, but every time she uttered one of those words, her voice would momentarily rise and she'd flash her eyes at us. It was bizarre.

I wondered if this was her way of dealing with words that were too uncomfortable for her genteel nature. Maybe, instead of shying away, she had decided she'd take the opposite tack and meet those words upfront, challenging anyone within earshot to question her choice of words. But then, she could have just chosen a common euphemism like 'loose motion' or 'gas.' Whatever it was, there was some deep and abstruse psychology at play here.

By this time, I could see that Gayathri was swaying on her heels under the assault, so I stepped in to assist her.

"This loose motion, madam, what colour was it? Did you notice?"

"Yes, that LOOSE SHIT was greenish in colour," answered Mrs. Visalakshi.

"And how frequently is Bobby passing gas as you mentioned?"

"He's FARTING several times a day."

"Yes, but can you tell us approximately how frequently he's having these episodes."

"Oh, he's just FARTING, FARTING, FARTING and SHITTING, SHITTING, SHITTING all day."

The eyes and the attitude were hitting me like a sonic boom.

"Riiiight madam," I answered. Turning to Gayathri, I asked if she agreed that it looked like a simple case of gastritis. She nodded in assent and we started preparing the drugs.

Mrs. Visalakshi kept up the barrage while Dr. Gayathri and I gave Bobby his shots.

"Why is Bobby FARTING?"

"Difficult to say for sure, madam. But it's probably something new he's picked up and eaten."

"He's always been eating rubbish. But he's never been FARTING like this before."

"Hmmm…"

"Is it normal for dogs to SHIT and FART at the same time?"

"Umm... it varies from case to case, Madam."

"FARTING and LOOSE SHIT all day…"

"Hmmm…"

"What are you doing to stop the FARTING?"

"Yes, madam. We've given Bobby an antacid shot, as well as a prescription for tablets to be mixed with his food. Please give it to him over the next week as advised... it should take care of both the loose motion and gas…"

"Okay, thank you to both of you, doctors."

Mrs. Visalakshi was smiling now and seemed to have shrunk back to her normal size. All the angst was gone and she was a gentle soul again.

"Say thank you to the doctors Bobby," she instructed her tail-wagging pet. And with a wave and many nods of thanks, she left, closing the door gently behind her.

The tension in the consulting room went out like a gust of wind. Gayathri finished washing her hands and turned to me.

"I'm going up for a cup of tea," she said.

"There are two or three patients waiting," I replied.

"Doesn't matter, they will wait. I NEED a cup of tea NOW," said Gayathri. Mrs. Visalakshi was proving to be a bad influence on my colleague.

"I'm going up. Coming or not?"

"I'll just wash up and follow you," I said.

And here, my long years of experience had once again come to my rescue. I knew that there were times when you simply did not argue with a girl even if she was a sweet-natured, pixie-type individual.

—

Every now and then, there would be a case that was not really a case at all. Or, it would be for such a trivial issue that I wondered why the parent bothered to take the effort and expense to bring their pet to the veterinary clinic.

An old couple with their pet dog came to the hospital one day during the monsoon season. It was a busy weekday and theirs was my first case of the morning. Their pet was a healthy-looking, smiley-faced German Shepherd cross. After I had lifted him up on the examination table, I asked the gentleman what the problem was.

"Roger is not playing like before, Doctor," he replied. His wife, standing behind and close to him like a shadow, nodded vigorously.

"Ummm... what exactly do you mean, sir? Is he not active like his usual self? Is he showing signs of fatigue?"

"No, no, all that is fine. He is very active, running around the compound of our house."

His wife nodded her head earnestly behind him. They seemed to be in their seventies and I felt she must have been a nodding shadow to him for the fifty or so years of their marriage. She agreed with everything he said.

"He is not playing his favourite game with me like before, Doctor." Nod, nod, went his wife.

"And what game is that?"

"Earlier, I used to hold the tennis ball up in my hand like this," he said, demonstrating by lifting his arm all the way up.

"He used to jump *more than five-and-a-half feet* and catch it, Doctor," he said, emphasising the distance. No dolphin jumping clear out of the water would have impressed him as much as his pet dog jumping up to take that tennis ball out of his hand.

"And now?" I enquired.

"Now, he's not jumping at all, Doctor! I hold the ball up and call him and call him, but he just sits there, with no interest at all. Why, Doctor?"

Prima facie, it looked like there was absolutely nothing wrong with Roger... he was bright-eyed and showing a keen interest in all the activity around him in the OPD, but I decided to check.

"Hmmm...okay, let me take a look at Roger," I said.

I proceeded to carry out a thorough head-to-tail examination of my patient. I started by taking his temperature, then checked his mucosae, palpated the lymph nodes for any inflammation, palpated his abdomen, checked his skin condition, auscultated his thorax for heart and lung sounds, checked his reflexes and flexed his limbs, to check for any signs of pain or stiffness.

There had been no episodes of vomiting or irregular motion. He was active, playful and eating well.

It was as I suspected. Roger was a perfectly healthy, happy dog.

"Have you ever considered, sir, that your dog is somewhat too intelligent for you? That he is bored and can't be bothered to humour you anymore?" I wanted to say.

But no sooner had the thought sprung up than I realised it was a mean thought. What, after all, did I know about this old couple's story? Roger was a big dog and it was clearly a strain for them to handle him. Why, then, had they brought him? Didn't they have any children or other family members they could ask for help? Just the fact that they were this old meant that they had seen their share of ups and downs in life. And even if there was no great story to their lives, their pet Roger was clearly their pride and joy now, and that was all that mattered.

Accordingly, I adjusted my attitude and rearranged my thoughts before addressing the couple.

"Roger is in good health, sir," I told them. "I've checked him over, and I don't see any problem."

"He's all right, Doctor?"

"Yes, he seems to be in perfect health and a happy dog too."

Both their faces creased into smiles of pleasure.

"Then, this not-jumping, Doctor?"

"Ah, yes, I think he just needs a change, sir. They are just like us... sometimes they get bored with a game and need some change. Why don't you try some other game? If you have a garden, you can try throwing the ball for him to fetch. May also give him some more exercise."

"Okay, Doctor, that's fine then...I will try that."

"And his coat is okay, Doctor? It looked a little dry to us... these past couple of weeks." His wife was into her nodding routine again.

His coat didn't look bad to me, but this was something that could be addressed without any unnecessary medication. It was a relief to have something concrete to work on.

"What are you feeding Roger?" I enquired.

"Only home food, Doctor. Chicken, fish sometimes, with rice. Sometimes we give bread, milk and biscuits."

"Hmm. Try knocking out the milk and biscuit treats, as they are known allergens. I'll give you a good dog shampoo, try that once every two weeks or so. I'll also prescribe a nutrient supplement that will help condition his coat," I said.

"Okay, Doctor, that is very kind of you," the old man replied.

And soon, my first appointment was finished. I wrote out a prescription and the bill. Thanking me profusely, the old couple walked out of the clinic with their pet.

In a way, it was nice to start the day with an easy case that did not require any heavy-duty diagnostics like X-Rays and blood tests. Sometimes in veterinary medicine it is not the animal that requires treatment, but the owners who come seeking reassurance.

—

Chippy was a honey-coloured mutt who could have been a geneticist's dream project, to unravel the multiple ancestral lines that made him. It was quite impossible to narrow his lineage down to even a few breeds. From certain angles, I thought I could detect cocker spaniel in his face, but if I looked at him from the other side, those features disappeared.

The fuzzy face pointed towards some terrier in his ancestry, but from the top, he looked like a warthog. After a few attempts at deciphering his roots, I gave up.

He was only about 12 kilos in weight, but built like a chunky tank, and was as strong as a little ox. When he came to the clinic, he'd always behave normally enough, walking quietly behind his owner. I'm convinced that but for his lunatic owner, Chippy was by nature a calm dog who could have spent his life looking on at the river of life flowing by with total equanimity.

Except that he had a parent. And she was completely cuckoo.

If ever there was a case of cloying love playing havoc with an animal's brain, this was it. To my mind, he had started out being a happy-go-lucky puppy. But the day he was adopted from the shelter by this woman, his fate was sealed. His brain had slowly turned to marshmallow.

He had come in that day for a fairly routine procedure. Chippy had a dodgy thyroid, so we wanted to take a blood sample and send it to the lab for a thyroid function test. When the patient is calm, the whole procedure can be completed in minutes.

In Chippy's case, the first task was to restrain him. With the ward boy holding his rump, I tried to put my hand under his sternum to lift him up on the examination table. "SNAP" went Chippy without warning and missed my hand by centimetres.

"Chippy... Chippy-O," said the lady sotto voce, as if she was coaxing him to come out from under the cupboard. Chippy paid her no heed. It was an appeal that I was to hear at least 50 times over the consultation, always delivered in that same dull monotone.

"Bring the muzzle," I told the ward boy.

"Will it pain, Doctor?"

I didn't think that question was worth answering and, in any case, the muzzle had arrived.

"Make sure it's tied tightly," I told him grimly.

"Don't tie it too tight, Doctor. Can he breathe, Doctor?" This, for a plastic contraption that had more holes than effective solid parts, in case the dog really wanted to bite.

In those comics I used to read as a child, the character's thoughts were always picturised in little cumulus clouds over their heads. In a similar way I started playing out a dream sequence in my mind, where my silent words were released in clouds above.

'Kindly shut up, madam,' I said in my personal cumulus.

We finally managed to lift him on the table. Four people held him down, two holding the legs, one putting his weight on his shoulder, one holding the head.

By now, with her ineffectual fluttering in the background, the woman had transmitted her tension to Chippy and he thrashed about in impotent rage. Whatever we were doing to him, he didn't like it, and he just wanted to get away.

"HOLD HIM DOWN!" I yelled.

"Oh, oh... is it hurting him, Doctor? Chippy... Chippy-O."

"Can someone please hold his bloody leg still while I clip?"

"Ohhh... will his leg pain, Doctor? Chippy... Chippy-O."

The woman then stunned everyone by putting her hand through the muzzle and into Chippy's mouth.

"If you bite, it will pain mummy. Don't worry, Chippy. Mummy is here. Chippy? Chippy-O."

As everyone collectively rolled their eyes, my dream sequence became activated again. 'Go on, Chippy!' I said in a fresh new cumulus. 'Bite her fingers off!'

But coming back to reality, I said, "Okay, is everybody ready?"

"Doctor, please get it in one go…"

I gave her what I thought was a withering look. It was completely wasted on her.

"Chippy... Chippy-O."

"Okay, steady... Hold him still…" I pushed the needle in and there was a general sigh of relief because in spite of the jerking and by pure luck, I got the vein immediately. The red blood flowed beautifully into the tube. I attached the syringe and soon had a lovely 2 ml sample.

"Ohh… ohhh… Chippy... Chippy-O," came the now familiar chant.

Once it was done, the muzzle was untied gingerly and we all stepped back with alacrity as Chippy sprang up like a deer. With many "oohs" and "aahs" and "Chippy-Chippy-Os," she lifted him down. He never so much as looked up at her or wagged his tail or showed any sign whatsoever of registering her presence.

It was the kind of consultation where you would feel justified in charging treble. But it was finished and we were glad to have reached its end. As the woman walked out to the reception to pay the bill and the ward boy cleared the trays and started to clean the examination table, I slumped into my chair. When I looked out of the window, the woman had finished paying and was walking to the door with Chippy in tow. I felt for that poor animal. We only had to deal with that woman for the duration of the appointment, no matter how infuriating, how frustrating it was. Poor Chippy had to live with her…no wonder he had turned into a sociopath.

Chapter Fifteen

Equine Medicine in the Nilgiris

It was the end of what had been a draining day during which we had been in the field from 8.30 AM until 6.00 PM attending to horse cases. We had just got back to the farm, and exhausted, we flopped down on the stairs leading up to our rooms. Cups of tea were handed out, which did wonders to restore us back to life. But none of us had the energy to climb the ten steps to our rooms or do anything as dramatic as take that sorely needed shower.

The restrooms were in a small building just to one side of our quarters. The door opened and out came Gokul, our batchmate. He walked up to where Kashiram and I had collapsed and made a trenchant observation.

"Hey, there were urine spots on the seat," he announced. "You need to put the seat up when you use the toilet."

Kashiram looked at me. I looked at Kashiram. Then we both looked at Gokul silently.

'Really Gokul?' I thought. 'Can you just bloody let it go?'

But that was Gokul in a nutshell. Everyone would be dying around him, too exhausted to speak, or in fact use the restroom. But he would find urine spots on the seat and make damned sure he made his opinion heard.

It was the summer of 2018 and I was at Ootacamund, Ooty for short, where I had gone for a week-long training course on equine medicine with the World Veterinary Doctors (WVD) organisation. Started by a European veterinarian, the non-profit organisation has two main centres in India, one in Ooty and the other in Goa, where they train vets on small animal spay and neuter surgeries. Rabies and population control are two of the main areas of work for WVD, so one way of achieving this mission was by training young veterinarians in countries like India and Thailand, who will carry forward their work.

WVD had recently started a new programme on the basics of equine medicine and I had signed up. I have always been a little loopy about horses but had never really had a chance to be around them. Not while growing up in Chennai, nor sadly, at veterinary school, where we mostly got to see cows and goats at the farm clinics, and dogs and cats at the small animal hospital.

The night I arrived, I was shown up to the guest house next to the WVD hospital and Training Centre, where I was pleasantly surprised to see that I had been assigned to a single room. Right next to mine was a room that was being shared by two other Indian vets, while across the corridor was the third room where two foreign vets were staying. One was an equine specialist from England, and the other from Spain, who, I discovered to my delight, was a zoo vet.

Dr. Kashiram Poonia was from faraway Rajasthan and Dr. Gokul Rao, from Nellore, in Andhra Pradesh. As soon as I had put my bags down, they knocked on my open door with welcoming faces. Kashiram and Gokul had arrived a day earlier, so they had already got to know each other a little. It was soon time to walk down to the centre's dining room for dinner and the three of us formed a natural group. In the week that followed, we spent our free time in the evenings drinking tea, taking small walks, and eating meals together.

Kashiram had a finely developed rustic sense of humour, which had been honed by twenty years of service in the Rajasthan state government's rural veterinary service. He was most comfortable conversing in Hindi, which I am also conversant in. Gokul's Hindi, on the other hand, was rudimentary, but he was game to try. That entire week, I heard him talking to Kashiram in nothing but his broken Hindi. His quirky nature, however, meant that he was always at the receiving end of our banter.

We reported at 8.30 AM the next morning at the hospital's library for the start of the programme. That was where we first met the Director of the WVD-India, Dr. Gertrude Schmidt. She was from Germany and towered over all of us. After a quick round of introductions from the participants, Dr. Schmidt gave us a short talk on what WVD's goals were for India, and what we would be doing during the week.

Like me, my Indian colleagues all had very little experience with horses. Dr. Meredith, the equine specialist from the U.K., was there more to guide us than to learn. And Dr. Maribel, the zoo veterinarian from Spain, was there to get more experience with horses so that she could apply those skills on zebras and other equids at her zoo.

During that week, Dr. Schmidt was always with us, driving us in the WVD jeep to field locations where the pony owners had their wards, guiding and encouraging us with the cases, giving lectures on her laptop, and welcoming us to her home at the farm at Mavanalla, a two-hour drive from Ooty, where we spent the last two days of the course.

She seemed blessed with endless reserves of energy. While driving us on those winding single-lane hill roads, with mad honking drivers coming from the opposite side, she would have one eye on the road while engaging us in deep conversation. At the field sites, she was the puppet master, directing the pony owners, managing the cases, and answering our questions. WVD was kind enough to organise a dinner party for us on the penultimate day of our course, and Dr. Schmidt was the first to get out on the dance floor with her staff, to demonstrate the local Badaga dance.

Most of the time, I was left breathless just watching her.

That first day, we were driven to a disused railway office quarters that the District Collector had generously allowed WVD to use as the field clinic. Since Ooty is a hill station, it is a popular holiday destination and pony owners make a living by giving rides to tourists. As we drove up to the clinic, Dr. Schmidt called out to some pony owners on the way, telling them to spread the word that we would be seeing cases that day, and for people to bring their ponies up to be seen.

Once we reached and set up the tool box and supplies, it didn't take long for our first case to arrive. A small lad walked in leading a beautiful horse and told us that his father was on the way. Dad arrived two minutes later, and pointing at the mare's left hind foot, said that it was wounded.

"Right, who vants to try vound dressing?" asked Dr. Schmidt.

Looking around and not seeing any hands go up, I tentatively raised mine.

"Okay, come on," she said. "Let's collect vhat ve need."

We picked up some cotton swabs, gauze, saline to flush the wound, antiseptic creams, povidone iodine and tape. On top of being a ravishing beauty, the mare was very friendly, allowing us to touch and handle her without fuss. Squatting down at the mare's hind feet while the owner held her halter, Dr. Schmidt showed me how to flush the wound and apply the antiseptic, followed by layers of bandages. In a few minutes we were finished and, in the meanwhile, the others had carried out a physical on the patient.

"Madam, I would like to try doing a rectal," said my friend Kashiram. "It will be very useful for me, as I get a lot of camels that come for pregnancy testing."

"Okay, let's ask the owner," said Dr. Schmidt.

The owner was a kind man and, seeing that we were learning skills from the WVD team, he agreed with some trepidation. "She is like my baby," he said. "Please don't allow more than one or two people to do it," he requested, to which we agreed.

We gathered around the mare, and it was decided that Kashiram and one of the WVD vets would do the rectal examination. Since most of us had never seen or done a rectal on a horse before, Dr. Schmidt gave us a quick demonstration on how it was done.

She stepped up to the mare's left flank, next to her hind quarters. She inserted her right arm into a parturition glove and pretended to lather it liberally with liquid paraffin. Soon she was ready.

"First ve must cup our hands like so," she said, matching action to her words, and making a cone of her right hand. "Then, ve must put our hand inside…" she pretended to insert her gloved arm gently into the mare, moving it along the horse's side, so we could imagine it was inside the horse's rectum. "Then ve MUST NOT PUSH. The horse vill sometimes strain... then ve must vait. Once she stops straining, then ve gently push again… for today, it is enough if you get a feel for the colon and uterus lying below it."

She demonstrated, like a ballerina, with her body twisted and arm extended as if it was inside the horse's colon. It made for a dramatic picture, which I duly captured on my phone. When I later showed it to everyone, nobody laughed harder than Dr. Schmidt herself.

—

When attempting to minister to animals, two emotional states are essential: calmness and confidence. If you experience even a low level of tension when you approach your patient, they will pick it up, no matter how much you try to mask it. And of all animals, horses seem to pick up human vibrations quickest of all.

During our day at the farm, Dr. Schmidt had pencilled in the placement of naso-gastric tubes as lesson number one for the day. The farm boys brought in Rana, a two-year old white gelding, to the yard and we all gathered around to have a go.

First, Dr. Meredith, the equine expert, demonstrated how it was done, explaining the steps as she inserted the plastic tube that was basically like a small-bore hose pipe. It seemed simple enough when she did it.

Working with horses always requires two people at the minimum – one plays the role of the handler whose job is to restrain the patient, while the other carries out the planned procedure. To place a naso-gastric, the handler stands next to the patient's nose, holding on to its halter. The person who will be placing the naso-gastric then takes position on the other side of the horse, next to its nose, facing forward. If you are right-handed, you stand on the horse's left side, and you slide your right hand gently over the muzzle, use your index finger and thumb to feel inside the nostril and hold it open in a flared position. At the same time, you take the tube in your left hand, again between your fingers, and gently insert it into the nostril. There is an opening there into which you insert, and as you gently keep pushing, the tube goes smoothly into the nasal cavity, through the sinuses, into the oesophagus, and all the way to the stomach.

The whole procedure was finished in a minute and Dr. Meredith gently drew the tube out. Rana just stood there with no fuss.

My turn came soon, and I stepped up to Rana's face. I made my first mistake before I had even started, because I put my left hand on his nose with the tube in my right hand and stood there foolishly facing Rana's bum instead of forward.

I could see him eyeing me quizzically. If he had eyebrows, the left one would be raised. "Hello, Mr. FreshGrad," I could hear him thinking.

I turned around and tried again. This time, I got my position right and stood on the left side of his face, facing forward. Holding his left nostril as far open as possible with my right index finger and thumb, I pushed the tube gently into it with my left hand. And immediately hit what felt like a soft wall.

"It's blocked," I announced. "It's not going in."

"Yes, that's the nasal diverticulum," answered Dr. Meredith. "Push it down gently from that point with your index finger, you will feel the opening," she advised.

As you feel inside the nostril, the diverticulum is like a pouch, a cul-de-sac whose sole purpose in the mysterious ways of the universe is to frustrate inexperienced vets. It has no other anatomical or physiological function. Try as I might, I could not find the opening and kept hitting the diverticulum. And now, I was getting more tense by the second. It was around this point that Rana decided enough was enough. With one toss of his head, he sent my hands and the tube flying.

I retrieved the tube and washed it afresh. I tried one more time, and this time, Dr. Meredith also placed her hand over mine, trying to show me how to push the tube at the precise spot next to the diverticulum. The tube went into the trachea instead of the oesophagus and Rana started coughing. "Take it out! Take it out!!" urged Dr. Meredith and I hurriedly withdrew the offending tube.

My nerves were shredded and Rana lost all patience with me. He simply refused to stand still. Not content with tossing his head each time I tried to place the tube, he started stamping his feet and moving about.

"You have to approach your horse with confidence," said Dr. Meredith. "If you are hesitant, some horses will not allow you to work with them."

She tried one last time, by herself, but now Rana wouldn't even let her do it, continuously tossing his head, neighing, and dragging the handler this way and that like a scarecrow.

That was the end of the naso-gastric lesson, and a collective decision was taken to stop. As the handler led him out of the yard, Rana walked with a high-stepping gait and a head-toss of defiance, tail cocked high, his white mane flying this way and that.

"Bloody amateurs," I imagined I heard him say under his breath as he was led away past me.

—

Every day of the course brought something different. On the fourth day, a Thursday, we had an adventure and also saved a life.

While wrapping up some consultations at the Railway Quarters Field Clinic, Dr. Schmidt received a call that a pony was stuck in a swamp and needed help. We quickly packed up and headed out to the site.

It looked like a large open field in the middle of the town, but it was covered in weeds and was probably a riverbed which flowed with water during times of heavy rain. It was by the side of a busy town junction and was being used as a rubbish dump by shopkeepers and the general public. On the other side, a slum colony had sprung up, and there was a narrow path that led across the whole site. People walked to and fro and the kids from the slum were playing in some portions where it was not too overgrown with vegetation.

Somewhere close to the opposite bank of the riverbed, we spotted a mid-sized brown pony lying on its side.

"Right, there's the pony. Have ve got everything, ropes, medicine box? Let's go!" said Dr. Schmidt and we all climbed down the steep bank to the riverbed.

After we had crossed about half the distance on the path that everyone was using, we had to step off it to reach the pony... and immediately my foot sank into the ground up to my ankle. It really was a swamp, and the mud was a sticky, oozy, semi-solid clay. But on we went, trying to find clumps of grass to walk on. By the time we reached the pony, my scrub pants were caked in a layer of clay up to my knees.

Upon reaching the pony, we saw that she was stuck in a small pool of water. She must have walked over to drink or settled down for a wallow, only to find that she couldn't extricate herself later. The owner had also reached the spot and told us that she had been stuck for about ten hours. The pony was clearly exhausted after hours of struggle and simply lay there on her side.

"Okay, here is vhat ve vill do," said Dr. Schmidt to the owner. "First ve vill try to tie ropes near the back legs and try to pull her out okay? Then ve vill give medicines."

The owner agreed and we set about the process of getting the rope around the pony. She was lying in a position somewhat half in and half out of the small pool of water so that her rump was slightly elevated and outside.

With some effort, we managed to get the rope underneath her hind legs and anchored at the groin area, tucked into her inner hip.

"Okay, some of you need to go to the front and push, vhile others can pull," said Dr. Schmidt.

Gokul and I went to the front, while Kashiram and four others took the rope at the hind quarters.

"I vill give a count of three and you must pull and push at the same time, okay?" Dr. Schmidt instructed.

We nodded and were ready. "Right... ONE, TWO, THREE PULL!" came the call.

We placed our hands on the pony's shoulder and both Gokul and I pushed as hard as we could, while the others pulled.

The pony didn't budge. "Right, one more time," said Dr. Schmidt. "ONE, TWO, THREE!"

Again, the team at the back pulled and we pushed with all our might. Still the pony didn't move. She was stuck fast in the sticky mud.

Suddenly she raised her head and tried to bite. "Careful!" I yelled to Gokul as I jumped backwards.

"Be careful, sometimes she will bite," said the owner uselessly.

"Oh really?" replied Gokul with acid sarcasm that was completely wasted on the owner. "Thank you."

"We can't do like this, Madam," said the owner – he had turned from us and was addressing Dr. Schmidt. "Better we pull her tail and push at the other side."

He had a point. The rope method was not working. Either the rope was not positioned properly to gain sufficient traction, or the pony's position was too awkward for it to be effective.

"Okay, let's try your method," said Dr. Schmidt.

So again we tried, this time with the team at the pony's rear end holding on to various parts of her tail, while Gokul and I stood ready to push from the front.

One more time, Dr. Schmidt gave the call. "One, two, three... PULL!" she called.

And one more time we pushed, while our friends pulled for all they were worth on the pony's tail. And this time, I felt the slightest movement, as the pony's body came marginally clear of the hole's edge.

"Okay, this might vork! Come on, one more time, let's try again! Ready? One, two, three, PULL!" called Dr. Schmidt.

We pulled and pushed, and this time, the pony came a clear foot over the edge of the hole onto terra firma. After that, it was only a matter of taking breaks and repeating the manoeuvre until the pony had been pulled completely clear of the spot where she was stuck, to a place which gave us enough room to treat her.

We were all panting with the effort, and the sun had come out from behind the clouds. I could feel its heat on the back of my neck and had started sweating profusely.

A crowd had gathered, mostly composed of the urchins who had been playing on the riverbed and the people from the slum. There was also the grandstand on the road, where all passers-by had stopped whatever they were doing and wherever they were going, to watch this novel show.

But time was of the essence if we were to save the pony. She had already been lying there for ten-plus hours and was badly dehydrated. And, in fact, as we quickly determined what our plan of treatment would be, it emerged that tackling dehydration was pretty much all that was needed to be done.

Saline bottles and infusion lines were gathered from the medicine box and an intravenous line was quickly set up on the pony's jugular vein. One person held up the bottles while another squatted down by the side of the neck, holding the cannula in place on the jugular. Gunny sacks were procured from the housing colony, and covering the pony with them, we poured water on the sacks, to keep her cool and prevent further dehydration.

Gokul was first to take the neck position, to hold the cannula. After a few minutes, I noticed signs of strain on his face, and fit as he was, I could see that he was trying in vain to shift his position to give his hamstrings a break.

“Want me to take over?” I asked him. He nodded with a grateful smile and I squatted down to hold the line.

It was at this point that the pony’s foal, a scrawny looking thing, made its appearance at the banks of the swamp. Emerging from behind some bushes, it began to call anxiously, not knowing what we humans were doing to its mother.

Gokul, I, and Dr. Jayshree, the equine vet from WVD, took charge of the cannula, so that between the three of us, in rotation squats, we covered the infusion. Only after a good thirty to forty-five minutes and about three litres of fluids being infused into her veins, did the pony finally show signs of getting her strength back.

She began to stir, moving her neck and rump in an attempt to stand.

“Okay let’s all stand back. Let her get up on her own,” advised Dr. Schmidt. We stood up from our positions around the pony and took a few steps back.

With one final effort, the pony heaved herself up. At first, she brought only her head up with her forelegs out, and she rested a few minutes on her chest. Then, with one more effort, she raised herself up and stood wobbling on her legs. We watched as she took a few tentative steps and swayed around, and then, eventually stood still and surveyed her surroundings. I let out my breath in a sigh of relief.

Her owner placed a rough rope halter around her neck and led her to the pathway. Someone had procured a block of jaggery from somewhere, to give her the concentrated glucose shots that she sorely needed to get some energy back. I took a small chunk in my palm and waited my turn to feed the pony. When I eventually held my palm under her nose, it was good to feel the slobbery lips whooshing over my palm as they picked up the last crumbs.

This pony, I felt, was okay. She would make it.

It turned out that there was a reporter in the crowd. The next day, Dr. Schmidt showed us a local newspaper which had run the story. 'WVD Veterinary Team Saves Pony' read the headline, and a brief article followed, detailing the heroic efforts of the WVD team. It was definitely one of the highlights of the week.

—

An equine veterinarian's work necessitates an assortment of specialised tools, and even in college, one particular piece of equipment had always stood out for me. It was heavy, made of iron, and was about a foot or three long. There was a handle at one end, and a rectangular part at the other business end, connected by a rod. The rectangular piece was smooth on the outside and had a rough corrugated surface on the inside. I had seen different models with varying patterns on the inside surface.

It was called a rasper. And it was used for dentistry work on horses.

I had my introduction to equine dentistry during that week at Ooty. Dr. Meredith told us that it was a good idea to check horses' teeth every few months, especially the molars, as they tend to develop uneven surfaces, with jagged edges that, if left unattended, may cut the buccal surface.

Each time we went for our street clinics, the set of raspers were in the tool kit and we never came away without finding at least a handful of patients that needed some dental work.

I watched with fascination as Dr. Meredith first demonstrated how to file down equine molars. Horses have long faces and their mouths extend a goodish way behind their noses, hence the raspers with long handles.

The first step was to give the horse a mild dose of standing sedation, and two of us were always assigned to this task. Once the patient was sedated and standing quietly, the next step was to place the mouth gag in place. This is a metal tool not unlike a wrench – it is placed so that the two arms sit along the upper and lower teeth and then pulled open, so that the horse cannot suddenly bite the vet's hand.

Dr. Meredith then selected a rasper of suitable size from the bucket and started work. Inserting both hands into the patient's mouth, we could see her pulling and pushing the rasp back as she worked by touch on one of the back teeth.

"First feel the teeth and locate any sharp edges. Then you want to use your good hand to file those edges down. You have to be firm but gentle," she instructed.

Soon enough, I had my first dental case. A tall bay gelding, he stood quietly under sedation as I gloved up and picked out a rasper under the watchful eye of Dr. Meredith.

Putting both my arms into the mouth, I chose the right side first and felt with my left hand along the teeth. And yes, there was no doubt that one premolar and two molars had very sharp, raised edges, mostly on the buccal side... they felt like the hard, razor-sharp edges of rocks on the beach.

Now I inserted the rasp with my right hand and tried to reach the correct tooth, using my left hand as a guide. But to actually rasp, you have to remove your left hand, and this made me a little nervous, lest I rasped on the wrong spot and ground off the poor horse's gums.

Taking a deep breath, I started gingerly drawing the rasper back and forth like a carpenter working on filing down the edge of a wooden rafter. It was much tougher than it looked, and within seconds, I could feel the strain on my shoulders and arms.

Dr. Meredith had showed us how, when you do it correctly, you can actually see specks of the powdered tooth on the rasp. After a minute or two of effort, I drew out the rasp to check it. There was nothing on the surface.

"Try again," said Dr. Meredith.

Once again I put my left hand in, identified a tooth that had angry sharp edges, and inserted the rasper. Again I started filing what I hoped was the right tooth.

"Go all the way in, then draw out the rasper in one smooth motion instead of going back and forth," instructed Dr. Meredith.

I did as she said, and yes, this seemed to work better. As I kept pushing all the way in and drawing the rasper out, it felt like I was getting better purchase on the tooth. Once again, after a few minutes of shoulder-busting strain, I drew out the rasper and was delighted to see that, this time, I had actually filed some of the offending tooth down. A fine white powder had been left on the rasper.

Putting my hand in, I felt the tooth and the sharp edge was definitely smoothened down.

"Happy?" enquired Dr. Meredith. I nodded in reply.

"Right, let's have a look," she said, inserting her hand to feel the tooth I had just worked on. She picked up a rasper and went to work on it. After a few deft strokes, she stopped, and drawing out the rasper, she felt inside with her hand.

"There, go ahead and have a feel now," she said.

I put my hand in and felt along the side. Sure enough, that tooth felt even smoother now – the rock edge that had threatened to shear the poor horse's cheeks into shreds now felt more like a smooth sandstone. This is how they should feel, I thought to myself... a beautiful row of hypsodont teeth, all even, with rounded smooth edges.

Dr. Meredith had told us earlier that she had an ambulatory practice in rural Yorkshire. I was curious to know if horse owners there often asked for dental services.

"Do you do a lot of dental work in your practice in Yorkshire?" I asked her.

"Yes, I get a few cases every week," she replied. "I always take my tools along, because you never know... clients will call me for something else, and then, once I'm there, they'll ask if I wouldn't mind checking the teeth. But there are some vets there who are specialists... they work exclusively on dental cases, so we often refer cases to them."

I was struck by that whole picture of a vet who did only dental work. Driving from farm to farm, rasping, rasping away every day, although I am certain they did more complicated work on their patients' teeth than just filing down rough edges.

One thing was for sure – they would have very strong shoulders and arms.

—

On the last day, we led some of the ponies into the shed at the farm for basic farriery work on their hooves.

We were all sitting on makeshift stools and chairs around the shed, taking turns to work with the farrier. Dr. Mohan, the WVD vet, was attending to a wound on one of the ponies at the corner. The horse had been given the standard shot of Xylazine and Butorphanol as a mild sedative. Within minutes, his head began to drop and his phallus dropped in slow motion out of the prepuce. That is an indication that the patient is properly sedated and that it is safe to work on him.

Suddenly Gokul stepped up to the horse and bent down, putting his face needlessly close to the patient's genitals.

"Ohhh – there are ticks on the penis," he announced. How he had spotted the offending parasites from where he was sitting, I will never know. He then proceeded to pick them off with his ungloved hands.

I happened to look at Dr. Meredith by chance. A whole kaleidoscope of expressions chased themselves in full speed across her face...

first came alarm, then repulsion, shock, a half-smile, and some others that I couldn't identify.

Gokul, as usual, had just made my day.

Chapter Sixteen

Kittu

Kittu was a seven-month-old German Shepherd puppy who walked into the consultation room behind his family one Friday afternoon in December. I was struck by the appearance of his owners: they were a family of priests - poojaris in the local temple.

That first day, Kittu was brought in by two men, whom I assumed were brothers. They wore no footwear and had their long uncut hair tied up in thick buns. Large rudraksham pendants hung on their necks and they wore saffron-coloured veshtis. They had lines of sacred ash on their foreheads and their teeth were stained dark red because of their habit of chewing on betel leaves.

As Kittu was hoisted on the examination table, I began my examination by asking the usual questions. One of them did all the talking. He informed me that Kittu had been very listless all day and had vomited once in the morning.

Kittu was a friendly fellow and I examined him thoroughly,

going step-by-step – checking the temperature, examining his mucous membranes, listening to his heart and lung sounds, palpating his abdomen and checking for lymph nodes. All the while I kept asking the owner questions, hoping for some clue for the possible cause of his sickness.

There were no obvious abnormalities. So I decided that I would give Kittu a deworming tablet and check his blood parameters for any signs of tick fever, which we were seeing far too often in our patients. I drew some blood and sent it to the laboratory.

We had the results in fifteen minutes and it showed a borderline low platelet count at 165,000 as against the normal range for Indian dogs of 200,000–500,000. His WBC count was also high. After a quick consultation with the senior vet, who also came and examined Kittu, we decided not to take a chance and start treatment for tick fever. I set up an intravenous line and gave him a dose of Doxycycline, which was the drug of choice for this malady. I also wrote a prescription for the Doxy, discharged Kittu, and asked the owners to return in ten days for a repeat blood test and medicines, as the protocol was to give the course of the medicines for a full 28 days.

As it turned out, I didn't need to wait ten days to see Kittu again.

He was back in the consultation room the next morning. And this time, he didn't walk in, he was carried.

I was shocked to see how much he had deteriorated in just about twelve hours. His eyes seemed to have sunk in and he was breathing with difficulty. Vaguely I registered his owners telling me that he had had many bouts of bloody diarrhoea during the night. Forcing myself to switch on mentally, I told the attender boys to bring the oxygen immediately and we hooked him up to it, as a first step. I asked one of them to check his temperature while I got ready to set up an intravenous line.

His temperature was 105 degrees Fahrenheit, which was dangerously high. Within minutes we had fluids going into Kittu to help him fight off the shock of fluid loss due to diarrhoea and bleeding. I placed some cool wet towels over his body and had the nurse wrap up the IV infusion line around an ice pack, to help his body cool down as quickly as possible. We turned the air conditioning down to 20 degrees centigrade and moved his table close to two large fans to enable cooling by evaporation.

I had done everything possible to stabilise him, but I was sure that he was going to die on the table.

I was able to observe Kittu better now, and suddenly realised the awful odour that came from his diarrhoea-plastered body and coat. His fur hung in long strands off his rear and sides, reddish-brown and crusted over with his bloody faeces. His tail and bottom had turned black with dried faeces. Right there on the table, he expelled some more liquid that stank terribly from his inflamed intestines, and a small pool of dark red, almost-black diarrhoea formed on the table.

Kittu didn't have tick fever, he had severe gastroenteritis.

I asked the owner again whether Kittu had been vaccinated and the owner said that yes, it had been done at our hospital. In spite of that, I wondered if Kittu had contracted parvoviral enteritis. I suspected his stomach and intestines were completely ulcerated, causing the bleeding. This was also causing the intense diarrhoea and inability to eat or drink anything. I had been taught that the inoculation does not give one hundred per cent protection, but I wondered if this was a case of vaccine failure. We ran a parvo test on his blood sample and it came back negative. Then, the next step was to treat the severe diarrhoea and vomiting.

"Kittu is very seriously ill," I told the brother who did the talking. In south India, when you tell an owner that his pet is "serious," it's an indication to them that his or her pet may not survive.

"Oh, sering'e saar," replied the poojari. "Oh, okay sir." I didn't hear much emotion in his answer. It was a phrase he employed several times over the following week, always in the same neutral tone. But it didn't mean that they didn't care.

They did and were there twice every day. Usually the two brothers spent an hour or so with their pet.

Throughout the week that they visited, I never saw them overtly express their feelings or worries. Even when they visited, they mostly stood by and watched me as I treated Kittu, only occasionally talking to him, or giving his head a rub.

In any case, now that the diagnosis was made, the treatment protocol was quite clear. Kittu would need aggressive fluid therapy morning and night, antibiotics, anti-emetics, and some infusion of plasma to counter his symptoms of vomiting, diarrhoea, and blood loss.

A couple of hours later, we had finished the treatment for that morning. I asked the attenders to clean up our patient as best as possible while I turned to speak to the owners.

"That's all, sir," I told them. "We have given all the medicines for now and also given enough fluids. You can take Kittu home and bring him back in the evening for us to repeat the treatment. Don't give him any food or water, otherwise it will induce vomiting again."

"Oh, sering'e saar," the brother replied. "Would it be possible for you to keep him in the hospital, saar? The thing is, we have pooja duty during the morning and the evening at the temple, and it's too far for us to come twice a day," he said.

"Well, it's usually better for the pet to be at home, as they feel less stressed there. But if you have this problem, I can check if we can admit him," I replied.

I went over to the senior vet to discuss this development and get his clearance to admit the patient. I was under the impression that poojaris were generally not rich, so I pointed this out to him. I was worried that they might not be able to afford the cost of hospitalisation.

"Sir, the owners seem to be poojaris in the local temple," I said. "Do you think they can afford to admit their pet?"

He looked up at me and smiled wryly. "They have been bringing their pets here for the past thirteen years," he replied. "They never hesitate to spend any amount of money on their pets, or question us about the treatment. Just inform them that they should pay a Rs 5,000 deposit and what the daily charges for boarding are. I don't think there will be any problem."

After talking to the reception to make sure we had space in our kennels, I explained the charges to Kittu's owners. They agreed immediately and Kittu was taken to what would become his quarters for the next seven days.

During the week that followed, my days at the hospital started with Kittu. I would have one of the attenders bring him to the treatment room from his kennel and start treatment. Kittu got nothing to eat or drink those first few days, because even a few sips of water would result in vomiting.

The first couple of days we gave him over a litre of Lactated Ringer's isotonic fluids to counter his shock. After that, the level was reduced to about half while continuing his antibiotics, anti-emetics, and plasma infusions. Kittu remained in a state of extreme depression the first half of the week. He was too sick to respond to my touch or take an interest in his surroundings.

On the second day, I was nearly finished with his treatment by about 9.30 A.M. Only a little more of the fluids had to go into him before we could lift him down from the table and take him back to his kennel. I put my hand on his head and stroked it, feeling the bony skull. With an effort, Kittu lifted his head and pushed it into the crook of my elbow.

It was a gesture of trust and affection. But I didn't know if I could live up to his trust, and instead of feeling nice, I felt sad. I prayed that Kittu would pull through. There wasn't much more I could do.

On Wednesday morning, five days after he had been admitted, Kittu's entire family came to the hospital. Having just finished his morning treatment, I had escorted him back to his kennel. When I came out, they were standing in the reception area, waiting for me. The brother who did the talking introduced me to his family as the "...doctor who is taking care of Kittu."

As they enquired about his health and prognosis, their concern and worry for their pet was touching. I explained what we were trying to do and reiterated that Kittu was seriously ill.

"He will survive, right, Doctor?" the mother asked.

"We will do our best, madam," I answered. "Please pray for him."

With hands folded in a traditional namaskaram, they thanked me and left.

That day, the two brothers had brought packed curd mixed with rice to feed him. When I raised my eyebrow at him, the elder brother explained that they had brought some food since Kittu hadn't eaten anything for five days.

Since we had been pumping Kittu with antacids, anti-emetics, and antibiotics all these days, I decided it was worth a try. If he managed to keep the curd rice in, I would know he was getting better. They had brought a large tiffin box full of curd rice. I took out exactly five tablespoons and put it in the feeding bowl.

"We cannot offer more than this," I told them. "First let's try with this small amount and make sure he doesn't vomit. If he keeps it in, then we can slowly increase the amount."

"Oh, sering'e saar," came the standard reply.

At first, Kittu showed no interest in the curd rice, which was supposed to be his favourite food. But when the owners diluted it with a cup of water, he started licking it up. It looked like his thirst was more urgent than any hunger.

"Right, take him out for a small walk, then put him back in his kennel," I told the attenders as Kittu seemed to lose interest in the curd rice after eating a bit.

Five minutes later, one of them came and informed me that Kittu had vomited out a watery frothy liquid as soon as he was taken out. Feeling defeated, I walked over to his kennel and bent down to him for a moment. "Bloody hell, Kittu, why don't you stop vomiting?" I asked.

In reply, Kittu pushed his face into the crook of my elbow. Wearily I pushed him away and stood up. Picking up a black marker, I once again wrote the following on the notice board hanging outside his kennel: NO FOOD, NO WATER.

Kittu hung on somehow, and I had the first bit of positive news on Friday morning, a full week after I first saw him. The attenders informed me that there was no bloody diarrhoea in his kennel overnight, and he hadn't vomited. Every day, that was the first question I'd ask them when they brought my patient into the treatment room, and it had always been answered in the affirmative.

I told them to bring a can of dog food gravy, and we offered a small handful to Kittu. Kittu took one sniff at the food and then gobbled it down in half a second. For the first time, I allowed myself a tiny sliver of hope. But he was still not ready to go back to normal eating, I was sure of that… he had to be brought back from the brink slowly.

Accordingly, I set up his IV line and repeated his morning treatment. When his owners came visiting as usual, I told them the good news and also suggested we try offering Kittu some of his favourite curd rice in the afternoon.

They were on their phones immediately and Kittu's lunch of curd rice was arranged. I went about my morning duties that day with one part of my mind on Kittu. Soon it was time to try part two of the feeding experiment. The rest of the family arrived with the packed curd rice at around 12.30 PM and Kittu was brought out from his kennel. This time when the curd rice was offered to him in a bowl, he ate it with gusto.

"Just wait for about ten minutes, then I'll ask one of the attenders to take him out for a walk," I said to the brother who acted as the family's spokesman. "I want to see if he holds his food down."

"Oh, sering'e saar," he replied.

When the attender arrived to take Kittu out, I couldn't bear to wait inside the hospital. I had to see for myself, so I walked out behind them.

The attender walked Kittu around the hospital compound for about fifteen minutes with interludes where he ran circles around his family, sometimes putting his front legs up on the chest of the brother to whom he seemed most attached. Each time, the brother pushed him down laughingly saying, "Seri da, seri da." "Okay, okay." His affection for Kittu shone forth from his eyes and through his spectacles.

Kittu didn't pass any loose stools, nor did he bring up the curd rice. I was thrilled and informed his owners that we had most probably crossed the danger. But I wasn't about to take any silly chances.

"Let's keep a watch on him today," I said. "If he stays okay today, no vomit, no loose motion, you can take him home tomorrow."

"Oh, sering'e saar," replied the spokesman of the group.

Kittu was finally discharged the next day, which was Saturday evening. To my delight, he passed the previous day uneventfully, and on Saturday morning, the attenders told me that there was no vomit or loose stools in his kennel. That morning, he came walking jauntily into the treatment room and began exploring the corners as if it were his first day there.

He was lifted on to the examination table, and quietly submitted to my talk and probing hands. While getting his fluids and medications going, I realised with a pang that Kittu would be going home that day. I was thrilled that Kittu had recovered so well from such a serious condition, but I had grown attached to this quiet, lovable German Shepherd.

The brothers soon arrived and stood around his head as always.

"You can take him home in the evening," I told the brother who did all the talking.

"Oh, sering'e saar."

Even at this moment of joy, there were no big smiles or expressions of relief. But genuine happiness suffused the room.

During a quiet moment in the afternoon, I walked over to Kittu's kennel. I thought I'd just say a formal goodbye over the gate. But I ended up walking in and crushing myself into the little space in his kennel. Kittu loved it and wrapped himself around me as best as he could. I was about to stand up and leave, when he gave me his own special gesture of affection one last time. He pushed his snout in the crook of my elbow and looked up at me adoringly.

This time it felt great.

Chapter Seventeen

A Day at Work

One morning during the week before Diwali, I had just emerged from the changing rooms having donned my scrubs, when I heard a commotion in the examination room. There was a large fawn dog that looked like a cross between a boxer and a mastiff on the examination table.

There was a group of people crowding into the room and I rushed over to see if I could do anything to help. As I suspected, it was an emergency, and the dog seemed to be unresponsive. Dr. M was attending to the case and she had a couple of nurses helping her.

They were trying to resuscitate the patient. One nurse pumped the heart rhythmically while the other held an ambubag connected to an endotracheal tube and pumped oxygen into the patient in synchrony with her partner. Dr. M suddenly shouted, "C'mon Bruno!" and smacked the dog's face. Her teeth were dramatically clenched, accentuating the pointy jaw on her oval face.

"Pump! Pump!!" she shouted at the attender, "C'mon wake up Bruno!" she exhorted the patient to respond to her.

The owner was an old gentleman who hovered around with a tense, worried expression. Every so often, he bent down and whispered to his pet: "Bruno... Bruno... I'm here…"

I picked up the stethoscope that was hanging in its place on the wall and listened for a heartbeat. I could only hear silence. I looked up at my colleague and shook my head imperceptibly.

She responded by browbeating the four-foot tall nurse who had joined the animal shelter just the week before and who had graduated from the veterinary nursing course just one week before that.

"Go get the oxygen!" she yelled at her, sending the poor girl scurrying out of the room.

I heard later that Bruno had been brought in that morning for an acute onset of vomiting and debility. He had stood there, head hanging, in severe pain, with chest heaving with every breath. He had been rushed in for X-Rays which revealed the classic 'double bubble' stomach, with two blown up balloon-like parts separated by what looked like a band. It was an emergency that vets the world over recognise only too well. Bruno had GDV, or Gastric Dilatation and Volvulus.

GDV can theoretically affect any dog, but the ones that are most at risk are the large, deep-chested breeds like the Great Danes and Boxers. It usually happens after a large meal, if the dog goes for a run, or has some heavy exercise or excitement. Then, the stomach rolls inside the abdominal cavity and twists on itself.

This has disastrous consequences. Due to the build-up of gas inside the throttled organ, it starts bloating and presses on the lungs, making breathing difficult. The spleen which lies over the stomach can also get twisted. The bloated stomach can rupture, causing quick death. Ultimately, there is circulatory failure and the animal goes into shock. It will die if the GDV is not resolved.

I placed my hand just under the upper thigh to feel for a femoral pulse and I thought I could feel the slightest rhythmic movement there. It was so faint that I wondered if I was really feeling it.

"I think there is a pulse!" I said loudly. "It's faint, but I think it's still there!!"

"Load the adrenaline, LOAD IT!" yelled Dr. M at the other nurse assisting her with the case, while simultaneously pumping the unresponsive heart.

She grabbed the syringe with adrenaline and made a few pokes into the thoracic cavity. She was trying to inject the adrenaline directly into the heart, which was the right thing to do in such an emergency. But it requires practice to know which ribs to use as markers and go in between to access the heart.

I watched as she jabbed one spot and withdrew the plunger to see if any blood gushed in and to confirm that she was in the heart. The syringe remained empty.

Withdrawing the needle, she jabbed at another spot about five centimetres away and again withdrew the plunger. Nothing. She tried a few more times, changing the insertion point at random but drawing a blank every time. In the end, she simply inserted the syringe and pushed down on the plunger. My guess was that the adrenaline was left swirling about somewhere in the thoracic cavity.

But it didn't really matter. My fingers were no longer feeling any pulse. With my other hand I was holding the stethoscope but my ears only heard complete silence. Bruno had died some minutes ago.

The time for subtlety was past.

"No heartbeat, no pulse," I announced loudly.

Dr. M's solution was to carry on her theatrics even further. She picked up a cannula, threw away the cap, and with a dramatic wind-up, she jabbed the needle directly into the bloated abdomen.

She wanted to impress the crowd and it seemed to work at least partly. There was a sharp hiss of shocked surprise from some of the people standing there.

Again, the approach wasn't wrong. At times it is possible to relieve the patient's discomfort by poking the bloated abdomen to release the gas inside and reducing the pressure on the lungs and heart. But it was done on presentation, not when the patient's condition had deteriorated so much. The doctor's ineffectual poking at the abdomen brought forth no gas. The patient was already dead.

She kept up the drama for a few more minutes, shouting "C'mon Bruno!" and slapping the dog's dead face but eventually she had to stop and inform the owner that his pet had died.

It was a lousy start to the day. Ever since I had joined the shelter, I had observed this lady. Her knowledge and skills were mediocre. Instead of identifying where she fell short and trying to rectify those areas, she used her gift of gab and a falsely confident air to convince pet owners. Many owners fell for her act and would ask that their pets be seen by her.

There were some that saw through her bravado and wrote unforgivingly scathing reviews of her service on the shelter's website. Dr. M didn't seem to care and carried on giving owners farcical advice and bullying the junior nurses and attenders.

The end of the day brought another fiasco. If Dr. M had taken the theatre of the absurd to an art form, Mr. Waseem's specialty lay in making pointless visits to the vet.

He was probably around 75 years old, and during his very first appointment with me, made it a point to describe the various successful businesses he had started, and some important people whom he counted as friends. He had made his fortune in the leather exports business and started several companies that were now managed by his sons. He was rich, but I suspect, bored out of his mind in his retirement. What probably made it a hundred times worse was the loss of the everyday fawning respect and subordination from his employees that his ego craved. As a result, his two dogs became the focus and purpose of his life.

They were both mongrels. One was fawn-coloured and called Ponni while the other was glossy black and called Kaali.

They were led in by Mr. Waseem's long-suffering Nepali manservant Kishan.

As Ponni was hoisted on the examination table, Mr. Waseem greeted me. "Good evening, Doctor," he said. "She's having a lot of phlegm.... for the past two days she's been coughing."

"Oh, is that so?" I replied. "Let me take a quick look, sir."

"Since yesterday, she's been coming and looking up at me every time I sit down, asking to be taken to the doctor..."

Being clueless about how to politely respond to that one, I let it go.

Ponni was an aggressive dog and she hated these frequent trips to the clinic. The same drama played out each time I had to examine her.

"Ponni, the doctor will see you now, no doing grr… grr…" Mr. Waseem would admonish his dog, wagging his finger in front of her face.

The moment my hand touched her back, Ponni would raise her lips in a snarl and start growling non-stop.

"Aiyy, no biting!" Kishan would say. Usually at this point, Ponni would suddenly twist around and have a go at my hand, amidst some useless shouting from Mr. Waseem.

I had learned the dog's behaviour quickly enough and had begun to jump back with perfect timing each time she snapped.

I checked her temperature and examined her as best as I could with Kishan holding her head. She was an old dog and showed some common signs seen in geriatric patients – she was eating less than she used to. She had an occasional cough and sometimes loose stools when she would go to the garden and instinctively eat grass. The thing is, she did not need medicines for any of those complaints, as I had tried to explain to her owner before.

On this visit too, she was in quite normal health. Sighing internally, I loaded an injection of a multivitamin and injected the poor animal. She took it, as she did each time, with continuous growling complaints.

Next, it was time to see Kaali. He was also a grumpy individual and we had to muzzle him each time before examining him.

"He's been itching terribly, Doctor," said Mr. Waseem. "And he has started smelling really bad," he added.

I ran my hand against the direction of the fur and observed the beautiful whitish pink skin underneath. Kaali's black coat was as glossy as a panther's. My nose was inches away from my patient and I couldn't smell anything.

I was squatting down by the dog and looked up at Kishan who was standing on the other side of the dog, with his back to his boss. "Has he been itching a lot?" I asked him in Hindi.

Smiling conspiratorially, he shook his head just a little.

So there was no smell and there was no itching. The poor dog had been dragged to the clinic for nothing. But I knew that Mr. Waseem wouldn't be satisfied with anything less than some injections. The question was which placebo would be the most benign.

I chose another multivitamin and jabbed the long-suffering dog who took it without fuss. "Say thank you to the doctor," said Mr. Waseem to his dog, who couldn't wait to get off the table and out of this torture chamber. Kishan had to restrain him from jumping down.

"I'll bring them again next week Doctor," said Mr. Waseem, as he pulled out his wallet to pay the bill.

"Really, there should be no need, sir," I replied. "I have given them their shots which should make them feel better."

"Oh," came the reply. "But Ponni especially asks to come and see you, Doctor."

"Yes, yes. But these visits are also stressing them out, sir. Better you give them medicines at home."

"But they refuse to take any medicines. Spit out everything."

"Hmmm…"

"And Kaali's coat starts smelling so much... he sleeps on my bed you see…"

"Sir, just have Kishan brush him for ten minutes every day... that will solve his coat issue much better than any injection I give him."

"Okay, Doctor," he replied, but he was already at the door and I could see that nothing I said was registering with him.

"Okay, good night, Doctor, I will come again next week," he said and left.

I couldn't help thinking that he and Dr. M would have got along famously. He would be at once thrilled and entertained by her vacuous and flowery explanations plus unnecessary diagnostics for the imagined ailments of his pets. She, on the other hand would have enjoyed his weekly visits, the willing ear to her loud talk and would have a client who liked and praised her work.

They were made for each other.

—

My last clients for the day were a smiling couple, who I later found out were Mr. Mahadevan and his wife Saraswati. The basket they carried into the examination room was emitting some loud mewing, and I guessed my new cat patient was not a shy individual.

With cats, we always take extra precautions, and I requested the clinic manager to lock the front door. On a couple of occasions, I had seen cats getting spooked and bolting. One had got lost, never to be found again, because she ran out to the road and just took off in fear. It was impossible to predict what could frighten them... a sudden noise, a dog, the sights and smells of the hospital.

So, in this case, before my clients extricated their cat, I asked them what the problem was.

"No problem as such, Doc," Mr. Mahadevan said. "We just brought our cat home a fortnight ago and we would like to start her vaccinations."

"Okay, we can do that," I replied and asked the standard questions about the cat's gender, age, behaviour, and activity levels before examining my patient.

The Mahadevans had rescued their pet at their apartment complex from underneath a car's engine about a month ago. It sounded like the rescue was just in time too, because the poor little furball was being attacked by crows. She had either wandered away from her family, or her mother had met with some misfortune. They had asked all the neighbours and searched the area for her without luck. Some neighbours told them that they had seen the cat with its mother a few days ago, but she seemed to have disappeared.

They opened the lid and a beautiful ginger-and-white kitten popped her head up. She looked at me intently for a few seconds and then surveyed this new place that she had been brought to. In a trice, she jumped gracefully out of her basket and walked up and down the examination table, tail high in the air.

She was a typical feline, filled with curiosity from whiskers to the tip of her tail. Her parents looked on with pride and love in equal measure as she took a sudden leap onto the top of the fridge. From there it was onto the shelves where I kept my intravenous fluids, and then down to the sofa.

"Better catch her before she knocks down all my medicine bottles, sir," I told my clients. They laughingly caught their pet and placed her on the examination table again.

She was very friendly and submitted to my handling with loud purrs of pleasure. She was in good health and I turned around to pick out the vaccine vials from the refrigerator. The clinic manager had come into the room, curious to see this new patient, and before he knew what was happening, she jumped onto his shoulder, making him exclaim in surprise and pleasure.

But that was her friendly self. She had a different side to her personality as we soon found out.

To vaccinate a cat, they have to be restrained. As I didn't have any helpers in that clinic and the clinic manager wasn't trained in handling animals, I usually asked the owners to help me.

I asked Mr. Mahadevan if he and his wife wouldn't mind holding their cat while I gave her the injection of vaccine. They readily agreed...but as soon as they hugged her close and held her legs, she sensed something was up and underwent an immediate transformation into a wildcat.

Twisting and contorting her body as only a cat can, she became a fireball of sharp needle-point teeth and claws. Giving a vaccination shot is one of the simplest procedures in veterinary medicine. All the vet has to do is insert the needle under a suitable area of the skin and inject the liquid vaccine subcutaneously. It is simple enough that students are routinely given this responsibility.

But with this patient, it was a struggle as she would not stand still even for a few seconds. It took several minutes to inject the vaccine.

"Right, it's done!" I said, as soon as the liquid was injected. "Put her straight back into her basket!!"

They put her in and shut the lid and we took a look at ourselves. We had emerged from the encounter looking like Tintin and Captain Haddock after one of their adventures. Hair all standing up, eyes popping, clothes all torn and arms marked by scratches.

The cat, for her part, had gone completely quiet inside the basket. No doubt, she was examining herself too.

"Sorry you both got scratched," I said.

"It's all right, Doctor," replied Mr. Mahadevan. "She's our daughter, so we have to accept these scratches." This was said with a smile at his wife, who responded with a smile in return.

But this was only the first of a series of four necessary vaccinations, and I knew this couldn't go on. It wasn't just about the risk, no, the total predictability of getting scratched and bitten again, but I was miffed at how unprofessional the whole episode had turned out to be. Besides, it was dangerous... if she got this stressed each time she visited my clinic, the danger of her escaping was that much greater. No doubt, the experience of being separated from her mother and almost being killed by crows had made this cat mistrustful of people outside her family.

One of the recommended methods to restrain such feisty cats is to wrap them up in a Turkish towel, so that their bodies and legs are kept inside the towel with only their heads outside. This protects the handler from being scratched, while keeping the patient relatively immobile.

"We cannot go through this whole process again," I told the harassed owners. "Can you bring a good, thick Turkish towel next time?"

"Yes, we will," replied Mrs. Saraswati. Her husband nodded, his eyes wide behind his spectacles.

As it turned out, I found an even better solution. The next day, I went searching in the storeroom for a solution. I was looking for a restraining container of some sort, something small that we could use to put the cat in and then close it up. I sensed that a towel may also fail in this cat's case.

After about fifteen minutes I found just what I was looking for. It was a bag, but apparently designed for cats just like my patient. The material was nylon and it was bright blue. It was like any other carry bag, except that it had special openings and zippers to facilitate working with uncooperative cats. There was a round opening at one end, with a Velcro flap that would hold the head. The top had a strong zipper that could be closed once the cat was inside. And small zippered openings were strategically placed on the sides, to open and access the skin. It was a work of art and I loved it.

The next time Mr. Mahadevan and his wife brought their cat in, I was ready.

As soon as they walked in, I asked the manager to lock the front door. I requested him to keep watch and ask other clients to wait outside until we had finished with this cat.

"We have brought a towel," Mr. Mahadevan said, smiling broadly as usual.

I waved it aside. "Just wait, sir," I told him. "I have a special solution for your cat."

With a finger on my lips indicating for them to be quiet, I gestured that they should place the basket with their cat inside, on the examination table. Next, I brought out the blue cat bag and placed it next to the basket.

"I will first load the vaccine," I said to them in a low voice. "Then, once we have everything ready, I will make a sign, and I'd like you to calmly, but quickly transfer your cat into this bag. We must work quickly to zip her inside before she realises what's going on, okay? And no talking until she's inside."

They nodded in agreement and I put Operation Spitfire into motion. Nobody spoke while I silently loaded my one cc syringe with the next vaccine that she was due for. Next, I motioned with my hand to make sure they were ready and I opened the cat bag, keeping the top lid as wide as possible.

I gestured that they could transfer their cat. Silently Mr. Mahadevan opened the lid of their basket, lifted out their cat, and placed her in the bag in one smooth motion. I quickly closed the Velcro lid around her head and zipped up the top. She was in. Next, I opened a zip along her flank, gripped the skin that was visible there, and injected.

The cat protested loudly, but there was nothing she could do about it.

"That's it," I told her parents. "You can put her back in her basket."

The operation was a success. The cat had got her vaccination with the least amount of fuss and we had emerged from it without being bitten or scratched.

"Thank you, Doctor," said Mrs. Saraswati. "That was sooo much better than last time."

"Yes," I smiled back at them. "This is how we'll do it in future also."

She was a true Jekyll-and-Hyde character, this cat, and I belatedly asked the couple what they had named her.

Mr. Mahadevan's face softened as he answered.

"We call her Angel," he said.

Chapter Eighteen

Vellaiyan

When I first met him, I thought the little white terrier-looking mongrel was one of the most sweet - natured dogs I had ever encountered. He had been christened Vellaiyan, which means 'The White One' in Tamil.

The local rescue group had brought him to our hospital after finding him lying on the side of a busy road. Nobody knew exactly what had happened, but the most likely thing was that he had been hit by a car. He lay there with his head low and eyes closed in obvious pain and trying not to move, but the moment I, or anyone, laid a hand on his head and spoke to him, the ears would go flat back on his head, and he would look up with a wide-mouthed smile, tail wagging in spite of his pain.

We tried to get him to stand and walk and he took a few shuffling steps, but it was not hard to see that it was very painful for him. He was given a sedative and a shot of opioid to relieve the pain before taking him for X-rays.

When the X-rays were ready, we all gathered around to look at the images of his back and hind legs and they told a sorry story. The poor dog's pelvis was broken clean through in two places and the left acetabulum, the socket of the hip where the head of the femur sits was fractured as well.

"Can you do an FHO on him?" asked the lady from the rescue group. The staff at the rescue had brought so many cases to us that they were familiar with medical procedures that we did frequently.

With dogs that suffer fractures or severe arthritis or dysplasia of their hips, sometimes vets can do what is known as a femoral head ostectomy (FHO). It's also done when there is a severe dislocation of the hip joint, when the femoral head slips out of the acetabulum and is not replaceable by mechanical force. As the name suggests, it involves surgically cutting off the head of the femur. What this does is help stop the pain and the continuous inflammation from bone spurs rubbing against each other. The muscles of the thigh then form what is known as a false joint and support movement of the leg. When I first saw patients that had undergone FHOs, I was amazed by how well they did. Looking at them walk and run, it was impossible to tell that their femoral heads had been lopped off.

Sadly, due to the multiple fractures, an FHO was not a viable option for Vellaiyan. We discussed another option with the rescue group, which was to have plate implants fixed into Vellaiyan's shattered pelvis; however, that would require referral to the Teaching Hospital at the veterinary college in Chennai, as it had to be done by specialists. The cost of transporting Vellaiyan to Chennai, as well as the cost of the surgery itself were beyond the shelter's budget.

In the end, we all agreed that the best way forward for the little dog would be to medically manage his case, until he regained some mobility, even though we expected that he would not have full range of motion on his left hind leg.

And so he was prescribed some strong antibiotics and Carprofen and sent back to the rescue organisation. We advised the lady who brought him in to bring him back in a week when Vellaiyan's leg would have healed a little more under the medications, so we could evaluate him again. Secondly if he was doing well and out of pain, then we could plan his castration surgery, which was standard practice for all rescues, before they found adoptive homes.

Vellaiyan came back to the shelter hospital ten days later. And as the cliche goes, there was good news and bad news. The good part was that his pain and inflammation seemed to be under control and there was no infection. The bad news was that his left hind leg had deteriorated. When I walked into the examination room, he was on the floor and he came up to me, tail wagging as usual and in no apparent discomfort. But his left hind leg trailed behind him uselessly. He was not putting any weight, or in fact, using it at all.

I lifted him onto the examination table to get a better look and it was not good at all. The accident must have damaged nerves in his lumbar spine that feed the hind leg, because it seemed to be paralysed. It looked like he had been dragging it these past ten days because there were wounds and ulcers on it and parts had become necrotic. It had not been possible to do a neurological assessment when he had come in the first time due to the great pain that he was in. Well, there was one conclusive test I could do now to assess nerve damage: check for a deep pain response.

I asked the nurse to hold Vellaiyan on his side while I picked up a pair of haemostats. Grasping his left foot, I grasped his middle toe with it, and clamped down with ever increasing pressure. Pinching down on digits causes extreme pain and a healthy animal will react immediately. The little fellow showed no reaction. I called out his name and pressed down as hard as I could. Vellaiyan looked at me, but just continued wagging his tail.

There was no deep pain reflex. And now there was no doubt either. The nerves to the hind leg were damaged beyond repair. There was nothing we could do to save his leg. If we didn't do anything about it, he would continue to drag it behind him until it became completely necrotic and infected, eventually spreading the sepsis to his body.

There was no other option - the leg would have to be amputated. I called in my senior, Dr. Madan Kalvi to look at the patient. Over the past six months since I had joined the shelter, I had assisted him on numerous procedures and had learned a great deal from him. He did his assessment and asked me about my findings.

"Yes, I agree. No other option but to remove it," he said in his usual matter-of-fact way. He turned to the lady from the rescue organisation and explained what we had found to her. He told her that it was best not to delay and do the amputation the same day. Rescue organisations see so many trauma cases that this was nothing new to her. She immediately agreed and it was decided to carry out the surgery in the afternoon. Since we would have him under anaesthesia for what was going to be a relatively long procedure, we would also carry out the castration procedure on him at the same time.

After signing the authorisation forms, the lady took her leave and the little dog was taken to the hospital ward to await surgery.

I had watched one amputation while in my final year at veterinary college. Standing with my group of classmates, I had monitored the heart rate and assessed perfusion as the two professors had conducted the surgery. Amputation of a leg is a surprisingly lengthy operation due to the density of muscle and potential for serious bleeding from the network of blood vessels that supply the legs.

I put on my doctor's hat. This would be an interesting experience, I thought to myself. It would be just Dr. Madan Kalvi doing it and me assisting, not me standing with a group of fellow students trying to understand what was going on. I hoped that it would give me some insights on the surgery so that when at some point in the future, I had to do it, I would be somewhat prepared.

Dr. Madan Kalvi was sitting in the doctor's office which had what passed for the shelter's library — five shelves lined with reference books. I picked out Theresa and Fossum's 'Surgery of Small Animals,' and turned to the pages that covered amputation of the hind leg.

The notes and illustrations described the procedure in clear steps. "Transect the gracilis muscle and the caudal belly of the sartorius muscle on the medial side," I read. "Isolate and ligate the femoral vessels. Transect the pectineus muscle. Transect the quadriceps muscle proximal to the patella. Cut the biceps femoris at the same level as the quadriceps. Isolate and cut the sciatic nerve…" and so it went on.

It made for good reading and I was pleased with my preparation for the surgery. But sometimes too much enthusiasm can come back to bite you at inconvenient places. I put the tome down and looked up to see Dr. Madan Kalvi watching me. He had a glint in his eye that foretold dark clouds.

"Do you want to do it?" he asked without preamble.

My heart rate shot straight into hummingbird range as I felt a thrill of fear and challenge. By then I had done dozens of surgeries and felt vastly more confident in my surgical abilities than when I first started with the shelter six months ago. But an amputation? That was a whole different level.

But when you are offered the captaincy of your cricket team, do you say no? Saying that I was too scared to do it was not really an option.

"Okay," I replied, my heart fluttering.

"Don't worry, I will be there to help you," said Dr. Kalvi and that, really was that. I was going to attempt my first amputation in about an hour.

I went back to Theresa and Fossum and read the details of the amputation procedure with renewed vigour and not a little desperation.

It was soon time. The nurses had sedated and prepared the patient and he was on the surgery table with an IV line and fluids running. My mentor told me that he would do the castration before I got started on the amputation so that I could focus on it. I started scrubbing in, and he took less than ten minutes to do the castration.

It was time to start. We had decided to do it with the laser to minimize bleeding since the laser would cauterise blood vessels as I cut. As the patient was being prepared, I had marked the spot on the leg where I planned to cut, with a black marker. As I prepared now to start cutting I realised that in my nervousness I had made my mark a full joint down - next to the hock joint - instead of close to the knee.

Well, at least I had realised the error before cutting, I told myself. I turned on the laser and applied the beam at the correct spot, a few inches above the knee joint. It was important to leave enough space along with tissue and skin to achieve a good closure after the limb had been removed.

The laser cut through the skin and muscle and as I guided it first on the lateral side, and then lifting the leg, on the medial, I settled unconsciously into surgery mode. After that I simply concentrated and all nerves and thoughts faded into the background.

A few minutes into the procedure, I was dimly aware that Dr. Madan Kalvi had left the surgery suite. He did this routinely. He was a great believer in throwing inexperienced surgeons into the deep end and allowing them to work things out. But I knew that if things got really out of hand, I could send out an S.O.S. to him.

As I expected, the neat differentiation of muscles into their separate layers was difficult, if not impossible to follow while actually cutting. It just seemed like layer after layer of thick muscle that was much deeper than what you would expect from the outside. I soldiered on, cutting, clamping, ligating, swearing, and sewing as I went along. Once I had the femoral artery finally tied off and it stopped spurting blood at me and I also had the sciatic nerve cut, the femoral bone itself was exposed. I picked up the bone saw which looked like a steel comb and placed it on the bone. With about ten back-and-forth firm strokes, I felt it go through. The thigh bone was cut.

All that remained now was for me to sever the remaining muscle and tissue and close. Soon the leg was completely off and I used a rasp to smoothen down the bone edges before closure. My position was good, I had adequate tissue and skin to achieve a good closure. Sewing away, I went from deep to outer layers, closing muscle, then sub-cutaneous, and finally the skin layer.

At last I put my needle holder and suture down and stepped back to look up at the clock. The surgery had taken me a full two hours. I checked my closure and I thought it looked satisfactory. The sewed-up stump looked pretty good to me without any ugly blemishes, crooked sutures, or skin tags.

I gave instructions to the nurse on post-op care: a continuous infusion of fluids and electrolytes for the next 24 hours mixed with opioids for pain, antibiotic injections, sedatives, and one medication for inflammation, alongside the usual monitoring of the patient for mentation, swelling at the surgical site, feeding, and bowel movements.

There was nothing else for me to do for the little terrier for the moment. There was a mild feeling of elation as I called the shelter to give them an update. "Vellaiyan did well during the surgery, it all went smoothly," I told the lady who answered the phone. "Surgery just ended, he may take an hour or so to wake up." I made a conscious effort to keep my tone professionally neutral, as if I did amputations day in and day out.

I took a break to have a cup of tea and then started on the other scheduled routine surgeries which kept me busy for the rest of the day. Once I had finished my last procedure my thoughts turned to Vellaiyan again. I thought I would look in on my patient before leaving.

He had been put in a small enclosure in the small dog ward and I walked up to it. I am not sure what I expected, but upon looking at him, I felt a sudden shock like I had been eviscerated. It was like the bottom had suddenly dropped away from my stomach. During the surgery, I had probably been too focussed on doing it right, and even after the limb had been severed and lay on the side tray, the priority was to close up as well as I could, then to keep the patient pain-free and prevent the loss of fluids and heat.

To see him lying there with only a stitched-up stump where his left leg had been, was a shock to my senses. I was overwhelmed by what I had done, even if it was all for the little fellow's own good. He lay there with his eyes closed and head low, just like when he had first come in. I called his name, and just like before, he looked up, his tail gave a few sad wags, and he put his ears flat and opened his mouth in a silent smile.

I patted his head and spoke to him in a low voice. I knew that anything I was seeing now meant little due to the heavy sedatives and continuous drip opioids he was on, and that to a large extent masked the pain and discomfort he must have been feeling. The real picture would emerge on the morrow, when I planned to take him off the fluids and start tapering the medications down.

As if to confirm my thought, he gave a small cry of protest when I palpated the left thigh, to feel for any heat or swelling, classic signs of inflammation. "Sorry boy," I said, as I transferred my hand away from his leg to his head.

Well, there was nothing else for me to do. Trying to convince myself that things looked as good as they possibly could, I turned away and left the hospital.

I kept my phone by my side through that evening and night. In case of any complications, I knew that the nurse on night duty would call me. No calls came.

The next morning, as I walked into the hospital, I went straight to the overnight nurse even before putting my things down.

"How is Vellaiyan?" I asked her.

"He is fine Doctor," replied the nurse.

"Did he sleep through the night? Any crying? Did he eat?" I asked.

"He slept okay…also no crying, but he did not eat the food we offered last night," she replied.

"Okay, let me go have a look," I said as I walked into his ward and approached his enclosure.

The fact that he had not eaten told me that he was still in pain, in spite of the opioids. But he looked a little more chirpy this morning and to my relief, showed no reaction when I palpated his left thigh area. The best thing was, there was no swelling, no discharge from the sutures, and they looked clean and dry.

I had a strong feeling of relief as I walked back to talk to the nurse's station to discuss his plan of care for the day. It was all looking positive.

I gave instructions to keep him on fluids albeit at a reduced rate and to also taper down the opioids. "Offer him some food again in about two hours and take him out for about 10-15 minutes," I requested the nurse.

"We brought him to the ward at 2.00 P.M. yesterday after surgery, right?" I asked her.

Consulting her records, she said: "Yes, correct Doctor."

"Okay, then let's stop the fluids today at 2.00 P.M. and we will reassess at that point. If he is better by then, we can think of discharging today."

The nurse nodded her agreement. She said she would pass on my instructions to the day nurse before leaving.

I got busy with my patients and did not have a chance to walk by the intensive care ward again till noon.

One of the senior nurses was on duty that day. He was a local named Velmurugan and had been with the shelter for about thirty years. He not only took great care of patients, having learned nursing on the job, but was a Jack-of-all-trades and was the man everyone called for when some repairs were needed at the hospital, or when supplies needed to be ordered, or even when food had to be organised for a meeting.

"Good morning, Vel," I greeted him. "How is Vellaiyan?"

"Ohh he is doing very well Saar," he replied, immediately raising my spirits. "I took him out at about 10.00 A.M. and he stood there and passed urine for one whole minute. Then he started walking around and pulling on his leash."

"He is already trying to walk on three legs?" I asked.

“Yes-yes. He is a little off-balance, but able to walk. In a matter of two days, he will be walking easily,” said Velmurugan.

“Did he eat?” was my next question.

“Yes Saar, we gave him a full plate of chicken-rice and he gobbled it up!”

I grinned in delight.

“Right, it looks like he can go home tonight,” I said.

“Yes doctor,” agreed my trusted friend. “The shelter already called about one hour ago. They have found a family for him it seems.”

“Okay, tell them to come and pick him up at 4.00 P.M.,” I replied. “And Vel, stop his fluids immediately, he does not need it anymore. His last dose of morphine can be given now, then stop that also,” I said. “When he goes home we will send him with the clindamycin and carprofen alone,” I said.

“Okay Saar,” said Vel. “When they come to pick him up, I will come and call you.”

It was around 3.30 P.M., when Velmurugan came and informed me that someone had come to pick up the little dog.

As I walked up to the consultation room with him carrying Vellaiyan in his arms, I wondered what sort of family the little fellow was going to. Knocking on the door, we went in.

There was a gentleman sitting there by himself who looked up expectantly as we entered and greeted him. Although he returned our greeting, he had eyes only for Vellaiyan and his face seemed to light up when he saw him.

I made a quick assessment. Even though he was sitting, I could see that he was tall and wiry with the dark brown skin and raven black hair common to Tamilians. He wore an untucked checked shirt and loose khaki trousers. He seemed to be about forty-five or so and his hands rested on a walking stick laid across his thighs.

"I am Dr. Krishnaswamy," I introduced myself.

"My name is Ignacius," he replied.

"Where do you work sir?" I asked.

"I work as a supervisor at the government cashew nut processing factory," he replied. "I've been working there for the past fifteen years."

"Do you have any other pets at home?" was my next question.

"No doctor. I used to have a dog, but she passed away last year. She had been with me for twelve years, since she was a puppy," he answered. "I have my own house in Teachers colony, close to the factory," he added.

I explained to him that the patient had come to us through the shelter and confirmed that he wanted to adopt Vellaiyan through them.

"Yes," he replied. "I have been in touch with them for about four months now. I told them that I wanted a small-sized dog to keep with me. Yesterday they called and informed me that this dog was available and showed me his picture. I decided to take him."

"Okay, that is wonderful," I said. I explained that Vellaiyan had probably been in some kind of accident and why we had had to amputate the leg. I reassured him that dogs usually do very

well on three legs and can lead active happy lives. I told him that it might take him a few weeks to adapt to moving around on three legs.

"I know," came the answer.

"We did the surgery yesterday and he has done very well so far. But for the next two weeks, you must keep a close watch for any redness, swelling, or discharge from the sutures," I advised.

"Yes, I know," he replied.

"Initially it will be a little difficult for you to care for him. Whenever he wants to go to the bathroom, you must support his weight and prevent him from getting soiled. Otherwise that can lead to infection and complications," I said.

Ignacius merely nodded.

"Luckily they are not like us," I said. "They seem to not be too worried about losing a limb, they just get on with life and adapt very quickly. Unlike us, they don't suffer emotionally."

"Hmmm…" came the laconic response.

Now I was a little perturbed.

Normally owners reacted with worry when given the care of a postoperative amputee animal. Usually, they were completely unaware of the challenges of raising a tripod dog. This gent seemed very laissez-faire about the whole project.

Would he be able to give this poor dog a good home, I wondered.

"Do you have any questions about the care for this dog?" I asked.

"No doctor," was the reply.

"We are sending him home with one medicine for pain and inflammation. And one antibiotic. Even if you see Vellaiyan improving, you must make sure you complete the course of medicines, please don't stop giving them until they are finished," I said.

"Okay doctor," he said.

I couldn't keep my anxiety hidden any more.

"Normally people show a little more concern when they see a three-legged dog. Have you had any experience with handicapped animals before sir?" I blurted out.

"No doctor," he answered. And then with a smile, he added: "But don't worry, I will take good care of him." He gave his right leg a solid thwack with his walking stick and lifted the trouser leg.

He had a prosthetic leg. I had missed observing the boot which would have alerted me to the artificial Jaipur foot that he had strapped on to his leg.

"Ohh," I said, not knowing what else to say. Ignacius had sensed my doubt and he set about putting my mind at rest. He answered before I asked my next question.

"It happened eight years ago, one night as I was riding my scooter back home from work. It was raining and visibility was poor. I was passing the Anna statue circle when an Ambassador car hit me and ran off. The doctors tried to save my leg, but it had taken a direct hit. They told me it was too badly damaged, so they had to cut it off."

"Ohh, that's terrible," I said, somewhat lamely.

"At least I only lost my leg. I thanked God that I didn't lose my life," he said.

"Yes, that's true," I answered. "Were you able to continue your work at the factory without trouble?"

"Yes, initially it was very difficult," he said. "It took me nearly six months to accept the loss of my leg and learn to use this artificial one. I could not do many tasks at work also…but they are good people and they helped me slowly adapt, so now I'm working just like before. With God's grace, I am doing well now."

I had, in my brief time working at the shelter in Thoothukudi, observed this attitude of calm acceptance over and over again. This ability to look on the bright side of things, the stoic surrender to destiny, the offer of gratitude to God for his many blessings…it all came naturally to the folk of the deep south.

"After losing my dog last year, I felt a terrible emptiness in my life, Doctor," he went on. "She had been my best friend. Even with my family members around me, I could not come to terms with the loss. I lost all interest in things, it was affecting my work also. I was simply waking up everyday and going to work, but it all felt pointless."

"Yes, I know how hard it is to lose a pet," I said.

"Finally, my wife made me realise that it was the grief over losing Rani that was the cause of all my issues. After talking it over, we decided we would adopt another dog."

"It is good that you had enough time to get over your grief of losing your dog, and that you have discussed it with your wife," I replied. "It's always better to think carefully about the responsibility before adopting an animal."

"Yes, Doctor, we are both ready now to have another dog at home. But I should tell you, we only thought about a normal dog, and we wanted one that was small, similar to Rani. We never thought we would get a handicapped dog, just like me!" said Ignacius with a laugh.

Vel picked up the little terrier and handed him over to his new parent. Ignacius's face softened with delight the moment he had the dog on his lap and his smile grew wider by the second.

"Vellaiyaa…" he cooed to the little fellow as his hand continuously stroked Vellaiayan's head.

Vellaiayan smiled back up at Ignacius, with the ears-back, tail-wagging gesture that I had come to know so well.

The adoption papers were soon signed and free samples of flea-and-tick medication handed over to Ignacius. I took Vellaiyan from him, when he prepared to leave. Placing the sturdy walking stick in front of him, he placed his two hands on it, and with a practised effort, heaved his body upright out of the chair. Once he had steadied himself with his stick in one hand, I carefully handed Vellaiyan over and he tucked him under his arm.

He thanked me and Vel, shaking hands with us before turning to walk out of the hospital with his new friend. I could sense happiness and pride in every step.

As I watched the two of them walk away, I felt a reassuring sense of peace settle over me. The anguish over removing that dog's leg, the questions about whether we had done the best we could for him, the worry about the quality of life he would have, all fell away. The universe had plotted and conspired to bring this one-legged man and the tripod dog together and my role in their story had ended.

Epilogue

The first night that I arrived at Peradeniya is etched in my memory like it happened just yesterday. I had taken the train from Colombo to Peradeniya. En route, I received a call from the Dean who told me to alight at Sarasavi Uyana, the station that served the University. "Are you able to understand me?" he enquired. "The station is Sarasavi Uyana, don't go to Peradeniya station," he said, making sure I repeated the name to him before hanging up. I hopped off the train at a quaint station that seemed no more than fifty feet in length and immediately looked up at the wooden name board hanging from the rafters - yes, I was at the right place.

The Dean had kindly come to pick me up with some of his staff. They drove me to a small roadside cafeteria where I purchased a packed dinner and then dropped me off at one of the boy's hostels where temporary accommodation had been arranged.

After they left, and I had taken a bath, I decided to go for a walk to get a feel for this new place that was to be my home for the next four years.

Once outside the hostel building, I crossed the road and walked down a path I found on the opposite side. Judging by the few students I saw walking towards me, I guessed it led to the university. I had just enough time to see that I was walking onto a bridge of some sort, before the darkness set in and everything around me turned inky black. I walked a few paces further until I was on the bridge and then stopped. It was too dark to walk anymore and I could hear the sound of water rushing somewhere below. All of a sudden, I saw a hundred pinpoints of light dancing in the air wherever I looked. It took me a few moments to realise they were fireflies.

I was filled with a sense of wonder and it was as charming a welcome as I could have hoped for. I watched them, felt the cool breeze on my face, and listened to the water flowing beneath for several minutes before making my way back to the hostel.

It was only many months, perhaps even a year later, that I had the opportunity to visit that spot again, while I was on my way to the boy's hostel to meet my friends. It's called Akbar bridge and it connects the main campus on one side to the engineering faculty and boy's hostels on the other - the Mahaweli river flows timelessly below. On either bank, there is an explosion of majestic trees and undergrowth that jostle each other to hold their place and remind you that with all your roads and buildings and universities, you are but a fleeting tenant here. Troops of monkeys jump and screech in the upper branches and birds call and swoop above the water. It is a spot of unbelievable natural beauty.

If you would allow it, Akbar bridge helped you reach places deep within yourself that you didn't know existed.

Once I rediscovered it, I returned whenever I could to Akbar bridge. Even if I was on my way to my friend Makinthan's hostel room, I would always spend a few minutes on the bridge watching the Mahaweli flowing below, or listening to the monkeys and trees as their branches sang in the wind.

They say travel opens up our minds. True enough, but I feel that equally and perhaps more importantly, it helps us build bridges. Between places, between people, and between ways of thinking. Underneath the translucently thin surface epithelium, we are all the same. In my mind, Akbar bridge is a metaphor for the beautiful connections I made with my dear friends in class, with my teachers and host family, and with the shopkeeper of the kiosk down the road from my house. I feel privileged to have lived in Peradeniya, surely the crown jewel of natural beauty in the paradise called Sri Lanka.

We human beings are consumed by questions about our place and purpose in this world, about who we are. What we do for a living is but a small part of that equation. It is however, an important part and looking back some years later, I am grateful that I took the leap into the unknown in my attempt to answer a yearning that could no longer be ignored.

The path contained innumerable twists and turns and at several spots, it seemed silly to keep pushing on. If logic and practicality were the only foundations on which dreams were built, I should never have started at all. Life's nature seems to be to continually pose difficult questions to us. Once we understand and accept that, we allow ourselves a chance to enjoy the journey.

For me, it all started that night at Akbar bridge. I have no idea where it goes next, and actually what does it matter? No matter what happens, I can always find an Akbar bridge and wait for the fireflies to show up.

Author at Dutch Fort, Galle, Sri Lanka

About the Author

Anand Krishnaswamy grew up in the city of Chennai in south India. After a master's degree in agribusiness and working for more than ten years, he quit everything and went to attend veterinary college in Sri Lanka, thus fulfilling a childhood dream.

He lives and works in Florida. You can get in touch with him at the Goodreads website.

www.ingramcontent.com/pod-product-compliance
Ingram Content Group UK Ltd.
Pitfield, Milton Keynes, MK11 3LW, UK
UKHW041630190726
13854UKWH00006B/2412

9 789390 053971